"The Crisis of Spirituality"©

From Suffering to Passionate Devotional Service

by

Nicholas Carl Moore

Published by VisionQuest Publications, LLC

Printed in the United States of America

DEDICATION

This book is dedicated to the many Believers who wrestle with the daily pressure of ***"managing"*** their Spirituality. The ebb and flow of the preordained relationship between God and man was placed in the hands of the Holy Spirit (HS) many moons ago. The relationship is not to be managed by man. Just like any healthy relationship, the partnership must be based on trust and faith and under girded with love.

The HS is the spiritual conduit by which man is led into the Presence of God by faith. The role of man is simply ***submission*** (which is translated into "service" not "slavery") and ***obedience.***

Trying to manage your spirituality is a huge mistake! The HS does not need your help! The reason we try to posture for control of our emotional and spiritual lives is because we want to be ***"relevant"*** instead of ***"righteous."*** This is analogous to having four hands on the steering wheel with two drivers wanting to go their own separate way.

We are more passionate about being right with man than being right with God.

The result is ***"chaos."*** Chaos is defined as complete disorder and confusion.

That is what this book is about: recognizing the crisis of the Spirit, understanding the revelation of the HS and then pursuing the remedy to minimize suffering in your spiritual life in your quest for passionate devotional service in the marketplace.

"The Crisis of Spirituality"

INTRODUCTION

"The Mind, Body and Spirit in Crisis"

"Be anxious for nothing, but in everything by prayer and supplication, with thanksgiving, let your requests be made known to God; and the peace of God, which surpasses all understanding, will guard your hearts and minds through Christ Jesus."

(Philippians 4:6–7)

Hardship. Strife. Deprivation. Distress. Affliction. Trouble. Pain. Misery. Depression. Anxiety. Tribulation. Adversity. Poverty. Trials. Misfortune. Destitution. You can say it all a thousand different ways but at the end of the day when your butt is in a vice grip you are experiencing a crisis!

In each word mentioned above, I am certain that each one of us can attach our name to a few of them that would describe how we felt during a period of struggle in our lives. If you were fortunate enough to weather the storm and make it through to the other side where peace abides, you can now claim the victory in the Name of Jesus and share your story with those who are currently trapped in a quagmire of fear and hopelessness. No matter what your situation is, the simple answer is this; Don't panic, pray and ask God to intercede, thank Him for the testing of your faith and receive His peace to resolve your pain, quiet your mind and guard your heart.

The best night of sleep you will ever have is the night the Spirit of God shows up to inform you that He has silenced your creditors, healed your body, crushed your demons and delivered you from the fire. Amen

Nicholas Carl Moore, Author

November 2019 – Grand Cayman, Cayman Islands

FOREWORD

"The Departure from Spiritually Dead Works!"

"Therefore, leaving the discussion of the elementary principles of Christ, let us go on to perfection, not laying again the foundation of repentance from dead works and of faith toward God, of the doctrine of baptisms, of laying on of hands, of resurrection of the dead, and of eternal judgment. And this we will do if God permits. For it is impossible for those who were once enlightened, and have tasted the heavenly gift, and have become partakers of the Holy Spirit, and have tasted the good word of God and the powers of the age to come, if they fall away, to renew them again to repentance, since they crucify again for themselves the Son of God, and put Him to an open shame."

(Hebrews 6:1-6)

The peril of not progressing in the spirit is rooted and grounded in not allowing yourself to be used in activities in the Body of Christ (BOC) that have no profit for your soul. Stop wasting time in activities that have no scriptural foundation and sitting under teaching that is vexing to your spirit man.

Too many Chrisitians are ever learning but are never able to come to the knowledge of the truth (John 8); in other words, there is no noticeable change in their spiritual walk (lack of growth and maturity). Gossip and haughtiness will stonewall the HS every time. Many Believers have "itchy ears" meaning they love to "hear" stuff about other people and act like they are concerned about them when, in actuality, they can't wait to tell somebody ***"what Brother Johnson did to his wife."***

Dead works abide in the spirit of a man that craves the need to be recognized by man in order to do the will of God (1 Peter 2:15) which creates an environment whereby the Christian constantly loses his/her spiritual gain ("backsliding") and causes people to lose respect for them. We must all relinquish our administrative dead works; which is slothfulness in the administration of our personal responsibilities in our ministry, family, finances and occupations (being a good witness for Christ on the job). If we are to be fit for God's use in the marketplace, we must be good witnesses in and out of the House of God.

Finally, we must move from our position of comfort in sin to God's requirement of chastisement, righteousness and holiness leading to love, peace, joy, son ship and eternal life. Amen...

ABOUT THE AUTHOR

Nicholas Carl Moore is currently the Chief Executive Officer of MANdate Ministries in Charlotte, NC. MANdate is an Outreach Ministry dedicated to engaging and empowering the lives of homeless and incarcerated men. Mandate Ministries Uganda (MMU) is an outreach ministry in Kampala working with youth, inmates and families with disabled and abandoned youth.

Nick has a new website: http://ncm926.wix.com/nicholas-carl-moore- His other books include: (www.lulu.com/spotlight/ncm926)

"Why Most Black Churches Fail Most Black Men" (www.lulu.com)

"The Road to Damascus: Unveiling the Heart of a Man" (www.lulu.com)

"The Belligerent Christ" (www.lulu.com)

"Hope Peddlers" (www.lulu.com)

"No Ears to Hear" (www.lulu.com)

"Pathways 2 Truth: A Devotional for Hardcore Believers" (www.lulu.com)

"A Wolf in Wolf's Clothing" (www.lulu.com)

"Every Knee Must Bow: At the Name of Jesus" (www.lulu.com)

"The Anatomy of Faith: Remedies to Prevent Spiritual Flat Lining" (www.lulu.com)

"The Idol Factory: Who and What Do You Worship?" (www.lulu.com)

"The Perils of Tradition: The Only Way to See It Is to Get Out" (www.lulu.com)

"The Crisis of Spirituality"

"Understanding the Presence of God" (www.lulu.com)

"The Invisible Kingdom: Learning to See What God Sees" (www.lulu.com)

"Tearing Down the House of Rebellion" (www.lulu.com)

Listen to us at: ***"Pathways 2 Truth" Radio*** on www.blogtalkradio.com/mandate. P2T has a current archived library of more than 350 shows. Nick is on **Facebook** as "Nicholas Carl Moore Author" and on **Twitter** as "Nickmo926". **"Mandate Mantle"** can be found at www.mandatemantle.blogspot.com. Nick has written many articles for magazines and is a prolific public speaker.

"The Crisis of Spirituality"

TABLE OF CONTENTS

Chapter One:
The Crisis of Spirituality

"Therefore we do not lose heart. Even though our outward man is perishing, yet the inward man is being renewed day by day. For our light affliction, which is but for a moment, is working for us a far more exceeding and eternal weight of glory, while we do not look at the things which are seen, but at the things which are not seen. For the things which are seen are temporary, but the things which are not seen are eternal."

(2 Corinthians 4:16-18)

By definition, ***spirituality is the quality of being concerned with the human spirit or soul as opposed to material or physical things. It refers to a religious process of reformation which "aims to recover the original intent of mankind," oriented toward "the image of God."*** There are a myriad of different ways spirituality can impact an individual, family or group dynamic.

Fundamentally, most people make the connection with spirituality through some religious organization or affiliation. The ***crisis in spirituality*** usually arises when the individual is faced with some form of personal calamity, tragedy or catastrophe. The loss of a job, a fractured relationship, the pain of addiction or the death of a loved one can send a person off the deep end. However, it should be noted that in every instance, there is a synergy of cause and effect.

Was it fate that caused Larry to have that fatal car crash? Could it be that Bobby got cancer because he couldn't stop smoking? Am I deep in debt because I couldn't control my spending? Or, did Connie break up with me because I spent too much time with the fellas and not enough time with her? These are all examples of the outward man perishing. Perhaps it's ***fate*** (the unseen thing) or the inevitability of trouble in a person's life that causes us to *faint* (become discouraged).

Paul cautions us to be vigilant in times of trouble and transfer our fear, doubt and worry to the HS. He challenges us to put on His glory and have faith in God to deliver us out of trouble into a place of peace, love and joy.

The things which are unseen are things of the Spirit and reside in eternity. They are unleashed by the HS as ***"gifts"*** to those in the faith to derail the evil plots of the enemy. These gifts are heat seeking missiles created to destroy the works of the Kingdom of Darkness (KOD). ***Our spirits have been weaponized*** by the Holy Ghost to seek out and rescue the countless souls caught up in the ***crisis of spirituality.***

The Apostle Paul encourages us not to crumble under the pressure of our daily lives as our human bodies, independent of the dunamis power of the HS, are not equipped to resist the enemy. Paul calls this crisis in spirituality a ***"light affliction."*** In other words, we are not to internalize the troubles we face on a daily basis but we should turn them all over to the Lord. Our "trouble" prepares us for true ministry or passionate devotional service.

Our ability to exchange "beauty for ashes"(Isaiah 61:3) brings the ***"kabod"*** (Hebrew for "weight of the glory of God") front and center to establish us as citizens of His earthly kingdom. The kabod protects us and it corrects us. The kabod covers our sin with the Blood of Jesus and the creativeness of the HS to administer our lives with grace, peace and love. The kabod is essentially the ***Presence of God*** in all its fullness and glory (Philippians 4:19). His weightiness keeps us grounded and focused on our assignments on the earth.

As we are living in Christ, we are dying to ourselves. The spiritual crisis for many in the Body of Christ (BOC) is how to reconcile a ***"living death."*** It sounds like an oxymoron, but in the KOG the ability to live and die simultaneously can be accomplished through total submission to the power, leading and guiding of the HS.

Reconciling the Living Death

"For as many as are led by the Spirit of God, these are sons of God. For you did not receive the spirit of bondage again to fear, but you received the Spirit of adoption by whom we cry out, "Abba, Father." The Spirit Himself bears witness with our spirit that we are children of God,..."

(Romans 8:14-16)

It is God's obsession with us that prevents us from being consumed by ourselves. God's grace is a prevailing spirit in the earth realm and the glory for mankind is rooted in his willingness to die. The Book of Romans teaches us that the basis for advancement in the KOG is predicated on receiving the Spirit of adoption which jettisons the individual from ***stardom*** (kingdom of bastards) into sonship (kingdom of Light).

In this, we are sealed with the Blood of Jesus and grafted into the eternal Kingdom of Heaven (KOH). The new man will literally witness the shedding of sinful actions, thoughts and deeds in real time. He will become bold and fearless and fight diligently to extend the love of Christ to those locked in the bondage of darkness.

Successful transitioning to the living death is marked by your acceptance of the ***"cross"***(burden) God has already given to you. Maturing in the living death gets down to how acute your hearing is. You have to know by now that the enemy continually accuses the beloved and that he is going to try to convince you that your cross is a yoke that cannot be broken. Will you listen to the devil or will you ***"hear"*** what God is saying to you about your cross (Luke 9:23)?

Your cross is your rite of passage into the KOG. It is not only unavoidable but necessary. The cross and the living death are inextricably connected to one another and afford us the fellowship we desperately need with the Lord Jesus Christ. The crisis of spiritually, in this sense, will be prevented because the temporal will become eternal, the dead will become the living and the bastard will become a son. Amen.

Sonship Through the Spirit

"The Spirit Himself bears witness with our spirit that we are children of God, and if children, then heirs—heirs of God and joint heirs with Christ, if indeed we suffer with Him, that we may also be glorified together."

(Romans 8:16-17)

The capacity to ***suffer*** is not in me but the ability to endure suffering is placed throughout my spiritual DNA, not in my ***flesh (my mortal body and carnal mindset)***. The modern day church has painted the wrong picture of salvation that, in many instances, excludes the mantle of suffering. However, suffering is essential to ***increase*** (growing in spiritual maturity, wisdom and understanding as a son of God).

The KOG makes the unattractive attractive! Most people despise war, but war is a way of life in the KOG:

"For though we walk in the flesh, we do not war according to the flesh. For the weapons of our warfare are not carnal but mighty in God for pulling down strongholds, casting down arguments and every high thing that exalts itself against the knowledge of God, bringing every thought into captivity to the obedience of Christ...," (2 Corinthians 10:3-5).

The KOG is actively engaged in spiritual warfare against demonic systems, paradigms and philosophies. Our primary weapon is the Word of God. This Word is seminal in nature; it has life producing attributes to create and sustain life. It is innovative, imaginative, influential and groundbreaking (John 1:1-5):

"In the beginning was the Word, and the Word was with God, and the Word was God. He was in the beginning with God. All things were made through Him, and without Him nothing was made. In Him was life, and life was the light of men. And the light shines in the darkness, and the darkness did not comprehend it."

The HS implores us to take the fight to Goliath. Don't wait for him (his spirit of fear) to attack you. Processing God's Word will create separation between the true Believers and the hypocrites. It is critical that as you go out into the marketplace to fulfill your assignment of passionate devotional service that you are comfortable with not knowing the complete revelation of His plan. This action is called faith. Faith will give the Spiritual Gladiator peace. And it is the combination of faith and peace that will ***slow down the Potter's wheel*** (Jeremiah 18:1-11) as you grow towards perfection (chastisement) in Christ. Amen.

The Spirit of Temptation and Dominion

*"No temptation has overtaken you except as is common to man; but God is faithful, who will not allow you to be tempted beyond what you are able, but with the temptation will also make the **way of escape**, that you may be able to bear it."*

(1 Corinthians 10:13)

It is very easy to see who is not following the WOG. The HS will help you to see the unseen thing. It is manifested in both the person's character and their words and deeds. Words and deeds should not contradict one another; they have a symbiotic relationship. The only time words and deeds contradict one another is under the ***spirit***

of deception (lies, trickery and chicanery) in an attempt by the perpetrator to cause confusion and/or temptation.

Temptation is rooted in fear and it has a profound spirit of seduction (1 John 2:16): "*For all that is in the world—the lust of the flesh, the lust of the eyes, and the pride of life—is not of the Father but is of the world.*" Temptation will either paralyze you or make you run like the wind. The Apostle James wrote these words under the direction of the HS in his epistle 1:12-15, "*Blessed is the man who endures temptation; for when he has been approved, he will receive the crown of life which the Lord has promised to those who love Him. Let no one say when he is tempted, "I am tempted by God"; for God cannot be tempted by evil, nor does He Himself tempt anyone. But each one is tempted when he is drawn away by his own desires and enticed. Then, when desire has conceived, it gives birth to sin; and sin, when it is full-grown, brings forth death.*"

Faith and ***movement*** are intertwined in the spiritual man. Once you start moving, faith is activated. There is no crisis in movement (Numbers 13:30). Where are you moving from? ***You are moving from fear to faith.*** Fear is ***static*** (lacking movement, action or change). Faith is ***dynamic*** (characterized by constant change, activity or progress). In other words, faith is the immediate manifestation of movement.

The ***fall*** (to be captured or defeated; to pass into a specific state or condition) of Adam and Eve was a fall from ***dominion*** (sovereignty or control) not a fall from heaven. The modern day church has been a catalyst for keeping Christians in the ***"fall mentality"*** or the spirit of captivity and defeat. The fall mentality has blinded us from the ***KOG mandate*** God has placed in our spirits. The KOG mandate is Genesis 1:26:

*"Then God said, "Let Us make man in Our image, according to Our likeness; let them have **dominion** over the fish of the sea, over the birds of the air, and over the cattle, over all*

the earth and over every creeping thing that creeps on the earth."

The dominion mandate produces KOG citizens and the majority of Christians are not operating under a Kingdom mentality with a kingdom spirit. Those doing so are therefore denied access to the KOG. Many in the Body of Christ (BOC) have also chosen to live as beggars and reject the KOG mandate. Storytelling preachers are obsolete. Entire families are being devoured by fear, confusion and spiritual blindness. Christian citizens need and want spirit led leadership that will humbly serve the triune Godhead and teach God's people with power, authority and wisdom.

The KOG message offends the masses. What is the KOG message? It is the bold declaration that we are the sons of the Almighty God and have ***rulership*** over all things in the earth! It further protests that we are heirs to the KOG right now and the KOH that is to come. It tells us that our primary point of contact is the HS and not the devil. It warns us that we will suffer for the sake of Christ. It states to us that we must die to our selfish desires and it mandates that we must serve God's people in the marketplace.

The KOG has been an abstract concept to the BOC because too many Christians have been held hostage through blatant ignorance spewing from the pulpit. It is solely the presence of the HS that cultivates our ability to receive the life giving, life sustaining message of the KOG. The origin of the KOG message stands alone as this: ***"It is the perfect prototype of a government built upon righteous judgement (Isaiah 9:6-7)."***

All kingdoms on earth have failed in their attempts to imitate the perfect order of the KOG because they have tried to execute the plan without the "raw material" (wisdom, leading and guiding) of the HS. The redemptive work of Jesus Christ is this; to re-establish the KOG on earth which requires much more than salvation. Salvation is the genesis of your ambassadorship (your representing Christ in the earth). Represent (or "re-present") Christ over and over again because the current view and perspective of God and the faith have been totally diluted (watered down) as we mobilize KOG citizens to proclaim Christ as Lord and re-establish His kingdom as preeminent.

Accepting the brand for KOG citizenship versus subjection to the world's system is your individual choice. I am my own greatest obstacle from entering into the KOG or my greatest asset to advancing the KOG. I must realize that I am a weapon in this spiritual war and that I was created for His intended purpose. People are attracted to rulership, spirit-led government, dominion and power. They are attracted to the Christ in you (Colossians 1:27).

Through us, Christ will realign the BOC, the spiritual church and the KOG. Adam and Eve released the ***spirit of rebellion*** into the earth. Sin has warped and exaggerated the appropriate spirit (the HS) God has placed in us. But it is God that will allow temptation to be placed at your feet and then trust that you will allow the HS to do what He was created to do and that is to deliver you from the path of unrighteousness (Isaiah 40:4).

Chapter Two:
Spiritual Elevation Comes Through Opposition

"Therefore do not let sin reign in your mortal body, that you should obey it in its lusts. And do not present your members as instruments of unrighteousness to sin, but present yourselves to God as being alive from the dead, and your members as instruments of righteousness to God. For sin shall not have dominion over you, for you are not under law but under grace."

(Romans 6:12-14)

Paul was very clearly communicating to his audience that elevation in Christ by Believers will be fought vehemently by the Kingdom of Darkness (KOD) and that the prevailing spirit in that kingdom will use anything and everything to manipulate them into committing sin.

He further warned them not to submit their mortal bodies to be used as instruments of unrighteousness in sinful behavior but allow the HS to use them as instruments of righteousness yielded to God since they were no longer slaves to wickedness but covered by His unmerited grace through faith.

The forces of darkness will oppose the sons of light. Your name is of the utmost importance to God because your name is usually tied to your destiny. In the OT, the birth of a child was a major event, exceeded only by the name that was given to that child. My name is Nicholas and it means ***"victory of the people."*** My story is unique only to me. My path is clear. My assignment has been given to me. I am walking out my destiny in real time. I have the victory and I am free!

What is your perspective when someone resists you, defies you, resents you or refutes you? Do you get angry or frustrated and lose your cool or do you process the form of resistance and deflect it with what the WOG says? Does your faith dissolve under pressure like Alka-Seltzer in a warm glass of water or do you limp off into a corner somewhere to lick your wounds?

Paul clearly states that we as Believers are no longer under the law but ***under grace*** (subject to or serving it and receiving it). Just think about that for a moment. You are a servant of GRACE! Grace is now a part of your spiritual DNA. What is grace? In this sense, grace is the adjournment or interruption in your death sentence through faith. You have received a reprieve from God and your sin has been forgiven. Finally, grace is an ***extended period of time (eternal life)*** granted as ***special favo***r ***(the sacrifice of Jesus at Calvary)*** to the Believer..

The finished work of Christ has given us access to the resources of the Kingdom of Heaven (KOH). So as God elevates us spiritually, He reintroduces us. People who knew us (and/or opposed us) as one thing are shocked when they see the same body (physically) but not the same person (spiritually)! Amen...

The Spirit of Freedom

"Then Jesus said to those Jews who believed Him, "If you abide in My word, you are My disciples indeed. And you shall know the truth, and the truth shall make you free."

(John 8:31-32)

One of the greatest things about being a Believer is having the revelation knowledge of what ***freedom*** really means. The New Testament teaches us that we are slaves to sin and in bondage to the whims of the enemy. It further rents the veil of ignorance to show us our sin nature and the pitfalls leading to perdition.

The spirit of freedom has produced a legacy of peace. Too many Christians are operating in the wrong kingdom;

vacillating back and forth between the KOG and the KID as it suits them. In the process, they leave a little bit of their soul behind each time until there is nothing left for them to draw upon to resist the pull of those living in darkness. They are saddled in chains all the while thinking they are free.

This is the power of the ***spirit of deception;*** people think that they are free when they are actually in bondage. No matter what the devil says or what you might think, you are only free when the Son of God has made you free. The Gospel of John tells us clearly that if you commit sin, you are a slave of sin. ***If you are a slave, you cannot be free!*** If you are a slave, someone else owns you and dictates your every move. They can and will manipulate you into doing evil and wicked acts against the will of God.

Demonstration of wisdom and knowledge is paramount in the KOG. The WOG is an open book and the key to everlasting freedom. Jesus refers to Himself as the "Bread of Life" sent down from heaven (***manna*** that will give everlasting life). The manna He is referring to is the WOG (John 1). In this life there is a covenant between God and man tied directly to the sacrifice (death) of Jesus on Golgotha and the Resurrection of Christ. In this same life there is a promise of freedom that can only come to the Believer through the Blood of Jesus and the power of the HS. You will know and recognize this spirit as peace, love and joy in the HS: "*It is the Spirit who gives life; the flesh profits nothing. The words that I speak to you are spirit, and they are life. But there are some of you who do not believe." (John 6:63-64a)*

There is no crisis in the spirit of freedom but crisis in the spirit of death and bondage is rooted in unbelief. Freedom compels the Believer to get outside of the church walls and minister to God's people in the marketplace. By being boxed in a building (the physical church), Christians are not a threat to the enemy. The enemy cannot bind a ***free***

man (a ***believing spirit*** living for and through Christ) and he is impossible to contain. ***Belief*** *correlates to* ***freedom***. When Jesus said, *"But there are some of you who do not* ***believe***, *"* I believe what He was telling them in the Spirit was, *"But there are some of you who are not* ***free****!"* Selah *(pause, and meditate on that)...*

"Ex nihilo" (Latin for "Out of nothing")

"In the beginning God created the heavens and the earth. The earth was without form, and void; and darkness was on the face of the deep. And the ***Spirit of God was hovering*** *over the face of the waters. Then God said, "Let there be light"; and there was light. And God saw the light, that it was good; and God divided the light from the darkness."*

(Genesis 1:1–5)

In the beginning of creation, the Spirit of God was there casting its Presence over the earth. The Spirit was patient and obedient. It did not get ahead of God. The Spirit was anxious for nothing. Darkness preceded the existence of light. However, God did not call darkness "good." The very first words God spoke were, *"Let there be light,"* and immediately light appeared. ***I also believe at that very moment the KOG (Kingdom of Light) and the KID were established.*** He then declared that ***light was "good."*** Light was elevated through opposition from darkness. The paradigm of light and darkness would wage war for eternity over the souls of mankind. However, it is critical that you do not miss the point here in that ***darkness precedes ligh***t and that ***light is "good"*** to God.

What does this mean? In essence, your birth and life before Christ is analogous to darkness. All the wickedness you conjured up in your youth and adulthood, although it may have felt good and you most certainly enjoyed it, was not "good" to God. You were lost and mired in sin. All the funky stuff you can't talk about; that's the darkness God is referring to. As you fall further away from God and get into a position you cannot solve yourself, you realize the thing that you knew all along but were too arrogant and selfish to admit...I really need God to save my sorry ass! So then you cry out, and piss and moan and bark at the moon because you don't have a relationship with the Father.

Finally, you are at the only point where God will step in; the point of ***brokenness.*** This is the point where the light shines brightest and you are like the earth was at the beginning; both void and dark. Brokenness is the gateway to the light. And, just like the earth, the Light shined forth in your life and God said it was good.

The elevation of the sinner into sonship occurs after the sinner embraces darkness and wickedness only to have sin wrangled from its grasps by the spirit of light and goodness. This is a spiritual conflict that is in perpetual flux and turmoil. The battle is ugly and ruthless. The collateral damage is staggering and the toll on human flesh is unimaginable. In the final analysis, God divided the light from darkness settling the matter once for all.

The Kairos Spirit

In the Greek language, the word ***"kairos"*** means ***a time when conditions are right for the accomplishment of a crucial action; the opportune and decisive moment.*** In Genesis 1, I believe the Spirit of God was waiting for the opportune and decisive moment for the ***kairos spirit*** to be released into the earth realm. The creation of light was invoked by the kairos words (spirit) "Let there be.." to produce ex nihilo and initiate the birthing of the heavens and the earth.

"God spoke the universe into being out of nothing. God did not take eternally pre existing matter or substance and reshape or reconfigure it into the present world. His anointing (creative activity) is not like that of human artists. Think of

Michelangelo, who sculpted magnificent statues from stone. Michelangelo believed that he did not create a statue but released the figure from its stone prison. It is inconceivable that his statues could have created themselves without the work of a master sculptor.

Michelangelo's genius was his unique ability to reshape a block of stone into a magnificent figure. But he had to <u>start</u> with some substance or material. Similarly, Romare Bearden had to begin with his canvas and paints. His inventive brilliance was in working with materials already at his disposal. We call this creativity, but no one in this world has the power or ability to create something out of nothing. Only God can do that.

Every effect must have a cause. There are different kinds of causes. Aristotle, for example, differentiated between several kinds, using the example of a sculpture: its ***material cause*** *(out of which something comes) is the block of stone; its* ***instrumental cause*** *(the means by which the effect is brought to pass) is the chisel and hammer, instruments the sculptor uses to bring about the effect; its* ***formal cause*** *(the idea to which the effect must correspond) is the sketch used as the image is shaped; its* ***final cause*** *(the purpose for which it is made) is to beautify a building, honor a commission or fulfill a vision. Aristotle also distinguished between efficient and sufficient causes: the* ***efficient cause*** *is the sculptor, who actually brings about the sculpture; the* ***sufficient cause*** *is the power needed to bring the effect into being."*

When we read in 2 Corinthians 12:9:

"And He said to me, "My grace is ***sufficient*** *for you, for My strength is made perfect in weakness." Therefore most gladly I will rather boast in my infirmities, that the power of Christ may rest upon me."*

God is succinctly saying, "My grace is the power (the sufficient cause) that shows up every time your mortal mind, body and soul fails you. It (My grace) quickens (makes alive again) your body and spirit and brings love, peace and joy into being (the effect). My grace elevates you through clashes of opposition with the enemy." The Apostle Paul asserts that when we are hurting or suffering that we should not keep it to ourselves. The spiritual crisis of what we should do or not do in this sense is called ***pride*** (Lucifer) and ***pride is a spirit***. The WOG teaches us not to be concerned with what man thinks about us and that we should ***boast in our infirmities (shout it from the rooftops)*** so that the Lord God will respond quickly and dispatch His peace to rest upon us.

The Spirit of Overcoming

"Then Caleb quieted the people before Moses, and said, "Let us go up at once and take possession, for we are well able to ***overcome*** *it."*

(Numbers 13:30)

Caleb and Joshua were fed up with the murmuring and complaining of the people and the bad report coming from the other spies. In fact, I am sure they were very angry! Anger is a reasonable part of the engagement process that needs to be allowed. The key to the healing process is a release of emotions. Caleb was present with Moses for much of the way during their journey through the desert. He witnessed the power of what God said and did. So it was easy for him to make the bold declaration mentioned in Numbers 13:30.

God always wants our response to any situation to line up with the WOG (James 1:13-15). We are encouraged to ***"overcome" all things*** which is a ***kerygmatic*** word (an emphatic declaration to go and ***take*** the victory from the enemy). The Greek word for overcome is ***"hettao"*** (hayt-tah-o), #2274 Strong's Concordance; it means to vanquish; to struggle against, to subdue, to lord against (over); to control, to subjugate; exercise dominion over; to conquer, prevail, to get the victory.

There appears to be a dual meaning to this word. Another part of the definition of overcome further states, *"to be inferior; to be completely overcome by (someone or something), or to bow together."* It also has a ***causative effect*** in that the ***cause*** or first requirement is to submit to God's authority (see what God sees) and the ***effect*** will be that you overcome.

It is critical to understand that overcoming will not be absent of fear. The HS told me a long time ago that, ***"Fear loves companionship and is a selfish mistress."*** Uncertainty is the thing that many of us are afraid of. Overcoming is conquering the thing that my senses cannot detect in the natural realm. Fear paralyzes us and bridles our faith. It is necessary to maintain the proper posture in the Presence of God in order to overcome.

In the Gospel of Matthew 14:22-33, Jesus had directed His disciples to get into a boat and meet Him on the other side of the Sea of Galilee. You know the story, but I have a little different take on it. As Jesus was walking on the sea, I suggest to you that fear bridled the faith of the disciples. The men on the boat had to be saying, *"My eyes ain't lining up with what I'm seeing! Therefore my reality (flesh) keeps me from the Presence of God's reality (His Spirit) empowering Jesus to walk on top of the water."* Herein lies the psychology of the flesh:

1. Our first reaction is ***fear*** (in what we hear);
2. Our second reaction is ***disbelief*** (in what we see);
3. Our third reaction is ***doubt*** (in our ability to do a thing);
4. Our fourth reaction (and most devastating) is that we ***stop moving.***

Peter asked Jesus, *"Lord, if it is You, command me to come to You on the water."* Jesus answered, *"Come!"* This is a critical moment in our analysis of this teaching. Jesus' response was an ***open invitation to anyone*** on the boat to come to Him. It was not a specific response to Peter personally! How many times has Jesus commanded you to come over and you stopped moving because you were afraid?

What I believe Jesus was really saying in the Spirit was, *"Overcome!"* He was saying to Peter (rhetorically), *"Who told you to come?"* In other words, *"You knew it was Me walking on the sea. Who else could it be but Me? You recognized My voice and the power in My words, that is why you came down off the boat. But the* ***sound of the sea*** *was louder than the* ***sound of My voice*** *and you stopped because you became afraid (your faith stopped) when you could no longer* **hear** *Me (Romans 10:17)!"* Jesus' final thought in the spirit to Peter had to be, ***"You stopped because You think I AM dead!"***

The name, (I AM), signifies the active Presence of the person in the fullness of the revealed character. In short, Jesus was saying to everyone under the sound of His voice, *"If you want to come over...overcome!"* Selah...

Chapter Three:
The Spirit of Passionate Devotional Service

"He said to him again a second time, "Simon, son of Jonah, do you love Me?"He said to Him, "Yes, Lord; You know that I love You." He said to him, "Tend My sheep."

(John 21:16)

Devotion to serving God's people in the marketplace *(tending His sheep)* requires a deeply personal and passionate commitment. Service is simply ***passionate devotion***. In the Gospel of John, Jesus proclaims that conversion to the faith is manifested through the love one living in darkness feels from the one living in the light.

It is the job of the Believer to replicate the work of Christ with the sheep. This is called ***discipleship***. Service is not what we do in the way of Christian work, it is the embodiment of the Holy Spirit (HS) that has taken up residence in the heart, mind, body and soul of the true Believer. Service is also what we are to HIM, not what we do for HIM.

Discipleship is based on our commitment to the leading and guiding of the HS. There is no room for carnality in service. Carnality totally dilutes the effectiveness of the Word of God (WOG). A person in need or a person in pain won't know or perhaps understand the "words" you might be speaking over them from the WOG, but they will most certainly feel and discern the authenticity of love being shown to them.

If you are fake, they will take what you are giving to them, but they will reject you! The homeless person, ex-offender, addict or even co-worker will be able to sift through the lack of devotion they feel and see coming from you and the need they are seeking to fill in their lives will remain void. This would be an epic failure in the KOG!

Your source of devotion is directly correlated to your ability to say, ***"Now I see who Jesus is!"*** when touched by the HS. This process includes the spirit of ***recognition*** (the ability to discern the times), spirit of ***conviction*** (when your heart is pricked to move into repentance mode quickly) and the spirit of ***correction*** (willingness to humble yourself and accept the behavioral changes needed for you to ascend into sonship with the Father).

There is a caveat in the KOG. Many Christians want to be devoted to Jesus but not to the ***"cause"*** He started. His cause was to be obedient to the will of the Father; not the needs of men. That might sound contradictory to the teachings of Christ; but it is not. The needs of men should never take precedence over the will of God. That is why it is absolutely critical to develop a strong connection to the HS. The HS will never make a mistake in directing your spiritual path. He will always say what the Father would say. ***He is incapable of doing anything else.***

Serving the cause of humanity will lead to exhaustion, frustration and carnality in the Believer. Subsequently, your love may falter. However, if you are passionately devoted to Christ and His cause, you will be able to serve God's people tirelessly (John 12:24) with love, peace and joy in the HS.

Sorrow, Sin & Suffering in the Spirit

In the Gospel of John, Chapter 12:27-36, sorrow, sin and suffering all visited Jesus on the Cross at Calvary. Sorrow, sin and suffering are what all Christians have most in common with Christ, but they don't want to deal with it. God made no mistake in allowing them to visit us as well! I always say that ***God has reserved a time for every man when He will reveal Himself to that man and that man will know without a shadow of a doubt that it is God Almighty through the person of His HS that has made the visitation.***

Christ on the Cross is an amazing symbol. It makes a nice conversation piece. The biggest heathen in the world will wear a cross or have a tattoo of the crucifixion plastered all over his body. It doesn't mean anything if you don't know the real story (if you can't tell your story) of the symbiotic relationship between you and your Big Brother Jesus and how you were delivered from every manner of sin, evil and mayhem and that, by God's grace, you are still standing!

Sorrow burns up shallowness, but it does not always make a man better. The way to find yourself is in the fires of sorrow. Suffering either returns me to myself whole, complete, at peace, lacking nothing or it totally destroys me. Sin cultivates character. It either drives you closer to or farther away from the Father. The character derived by the man is either rooted in darkness or light.

Imagine being held captive for someone else's crime. Then being tortured, beaten and ridiculed by the very people you were sent to save. Those same people did not come to help you when they had the chance but rather chose to run and hide and save their own necks. Most of all, why would God, your Holy Father, stand idly by and do nothing to stop the heinous and bigoted slaughter of an innocent man? This is the ***chaos*** inextricably connected to the salvation, righteousness and deliverance of the innocents.

You must not miss this point! ***God Almighty was not grieved one iota that Jesus was killed on the Cross.*** In fact, it was premeditated and unavoidable! Even Jesus saw the *"big picture."* He had to repeat to Himself over and over again, *"If I don't die, they cannot live."*

God's masterplan for the salvation of man (**soteria** in Greek;

#4991 ***sōtēría*** *(from 4982 /sṓzō, "to save, rescue") – salvation, i.e. God's rescue which delivers believers out of destruction and into His safety)* requires that the man be roasted, stewed and barbecued in the fire (symbolic of purging). The man that has found himself in the fire and has survived it can now receive a brother or sister in trouble and provide ***nourishment*** (their personal testimony of deliverance from the fire) for their souls. The target of every righteous man is the salvation of his spirit man as it is the bridge to eternal life.

A man who has not been tested in the fire will be contentious and selfish. He will not have time for you and he will leave you alone for sorrow, sin and suffering to have its way with you! Selah...

Walking in the Spirit

"I say then: Walk in the Spirit, and you shall not fulfill the lust of the flesh. For the flesh lusts against the Spirit, and the Spirit against the flesh; and these are contrary to one another, so that you do not do the things that you wish. But if you are led by the Spirit, you are not under the law."

(Galatians 5:16-18)

Once again the Apostle Paul is giving us incredible revelation from the lips of the HS that would allow us to be righteous ambassadors for Christ in the marketplace. To do so you must habitually walk in the Spirit (by seeking Him and being responsive to His guidance) and you will be able to resist the sinful nature that responds impulsively to your desires without regard for God and His precepts. As we grow in faith, our pain transforms into passion. He cautions us not to leave one another without accountability to the Master and/or another brother or sister who is mature in Christ.

There is always a crisis in service. The sad reality is that most often the crisis is self induced. It usually boils down to time, talent and treasury. Is your life so busy that you can't be interrupted to volunteer at the homeless shelter or drop off food at the food bank? Have you had the opportunity to develop your "gifts"(talents) so that your service will not be drudgery or unfulfilling? And finally, is the reason that you don't, won't or can't serve because you are just too broke and stressed out?

Paul goes on to write in this scripture vv. 19-21:

*"Now **the works of the flesh are evident**, which are: adultery, fornication, uncleanness, lewdness, idolatry, sorcery, hatred, contentions, jealousies, outbursts of wrath, selfish ambitions, dissensions, heresies, envy, murders, drunkenness, revelries, and the like; of which I tell you beforehand, just as I also told you in time past, that those who practice such things will not inherit the kingdom of God."*

The crisis in walking in the Spirit is managing sin. The aforementioned scripture is a hall of fame list of sinful behavior that each one of us can hang our hats on. Thank God He didn't abandon us when we were at our lowest point and we called out for Him to rescue us. The HS retrained, reformed and repurposed us for goodness. Praise God that He stepped in to protect us from ourselves which afforded us the opportunity to inherit the KOG! The HS warns us not to practice sinful behavior (don't vacillate between good and evil). The two worlds that collide in the earth realm continually are the ***works of the devil and the fruit of the spirit*** *(vv.22-26):*

*"But the **fruit of the Spirit** is love, joy, peace, longsuffering, kindness, goodness, faithfulness, gentleness, self-control. Against such there is no law. And those who are Christ's have crucified the flesh with its passions and desires. If we live in the Spirit, let us also walk in the Spirit. Let us not*

become conceited, provoking one another, envying one another."

God wants us to have the fruit of the Spirit for this reason: "*For those whom He foreknew [and loved and chose beforehand], He also predestined to be conformed to the image of His Son [and ultimately share in His complete sanctification], so that He would be the firstborn [the most beloved and honored] among many believers." (Romans 8:29 AMP)*. The HS will labor until the image of Christ has been formed (taken up residence) in your spirit. There is nothing that can stop God from being glorified, especially sin.

Galatians 5:22 tells us that all of the **"fruit"** is perfected in Christ Jesus and the perfection of fruit allowed Him to manage the "gifts"of the HS without reproach or transgression. The gift of the HS is salvation (Acts 2:38) and is our supernatural ability to glorify the KOG whereby the Believer actually receives the HS Himself (not a diluted version of the HS)! Finally, the character of Christ is revealed through the fruit of the HS and that character is vested in the Presence and Power of the HS. However, I must caution you that a lack of spiritual maturity will stifle the ability of the Christian to operate the gifts effectively for the advancement of the KOG.

The Spirit of Patience

"My brethren, count it all joy when you fall into various trials, knowing that the testing of your faith produces patience. But let patience have its perfect work, that you may be perfect and complete, lacking nothing."

(James 1:2-4)

Boy oh boy, you need a whole lot of patience dealing with folks these days! Brother James said parenthetically, *"Don't trip when folks get on your nerves. It's a good thing because they are helping to mature you in faith and faith produces* ***patience (the capacity to accept or tolerate delay, trouble, or suffering without getting angry or upset).*** *Enjoy the process in the fire allowing patience to do what it does; making you faultless, exemplary and complete in the spirit."*

The epistle of James is a practical look at the life of a Believer. He embraced his audience with a heartfelt letter that captured the climate of the times perfectly and conveyed a very strong message of support for those who remained steadfast in the faith as well as an equally strong rebuke for those who did not. He was adamant that we endure the trials and tribulations that court our mortal bodies seemingly moment by moment and encouraged his listeners to immerse themselves in the bosom of Christ Jesus as the Savior of the world.

The meaning of patience transcends the idea of bearing trouble or affliction; it also includes the idea of remaining steadfast under pressure with a resolve that transforms torment into triumph. ***Perfection,*** in the spiritual sense, is deeper than the condition, state or quality of being free or as free as possible from all flaws or defects. I liken it to numismatics (the art of coin collecting) when an old coin is discovered and special care is taken to preserve the integrity of the coin so as not to debase it. The coin is then ***tested*** to affirm its authenticity. In this case, testing the coin is essential for purging and refining, not destruction. In the end, the numismatist (the HS) would declare whether or not the coin was genuine or a fake once it has gone through the fire (testing). The coin (new Believer) now becomes invaluable to the owner (God) and is put on display (a priceless witness for Christ) for all the world to see.

Patience and perfection have a symbiotic relationship. *The common denominator is* ***time****.* However, time is the ***enem***y of patience. Time is a crucial element in the temporal realm. It is omnipotent! But in the eternal realm, time is of no consequence. It is inert, powerless and meaningless. Time holds everyone hostage at one point or another creating feelings of fear, despair and helplessness.

But patience is a ***good and perfect gift*** from God. The good gift is predicated on the act of giving while the perfect gift denotes the actual gifts received. In short, the first expression emphasizes the goodness of receiving something from God, while the second outlines the perfect quality of anything God gives to us (the gifts). God's giving is perpetually good and His gifts are always perfect.

The Spirit of Engagement

"But you shall receive power when the Holy Spirit has come upon you; and you shall be witnesses to Me in Jerusalem, and in all Judea and Samaria, and to the end of the earth."

(Acts 1:8)

Everything we do must lead others to ***repentance***, not necessarily a ***decision*** (to accept Christ as Lord and Savior). The "crossing over" so to speak that fosters the decision of acceptance is solely in the hands of the Lord. The scramble for salvations is a bit of a crisis in the modern day church because the pressure is on to see how many people we can get saved. If we have a camp meeting and nobody accepts Jesus, the gathering is viewed as an abysmal failure.

Apostles in the NT church were more often than not missionaries. They weren't spiritual prima donnas carried around on the shoulders of slaves being fanned with giant ostrich feathers. These brothers did the grunt work (much of it on foot through very dangerous regions) to spread the Good News. They did it without fanfare going from house to house and city to city to engage and empower God's people. Many of the witnesses' names we will never know until the Great Day; but they do have a place in eternity. These great men relied solely on the Spirit to do the work of redemption and revival. They were only vessels to be used by God anyway He saw fit.

How many times have you been to a church and had the hireling preacher make multiple altar calls to guilt people into stepping out of the pews up to the front of the church? When you hear the declaration coming from the pulpit, *"The doors of the church are now open. Will you come? Will you receive the right hand of fellowship and open your heart and let Jesus come into your life? It doesn't matter what you've done, Jesus still loves you!"* The Christian church has a knack for wearing folks down. At this point in the service, you know the pastor is going to milk the situation for another 45 minutes to an hour! Is this experience really happening under the leadership of the HS?

What do we make of this? There are certainly times of genuine spiritual encounters, but in many of these instances, the spirit of engagement has been bastardized to the point of futility. I have witnessed this scenario too many times to count over the past twenty plus years in outreach ministry. I have worked with the homeless population since the late 90's and have anguished over the plethora of souls dashed by over ambitious Christians trying to ***save somebody*** and, quite frankly, didn't know what the hell they were doing!

There are rules of engagement in the KOG. You have to discern the times. You must exercise humility and grace when approaching a brother or sister in pain. You can't just roll up on somebody and break out the "Romans Road to Salvation" track you just memorized! No, no, no. It is imperative that we provoke the Spirit of Truth to lead the engagement and we must follow.

Paul taught them to embrace the ***spirit of self-examination.*** This spirit allows the judgement (chastisement) of the Lord freely and accepts the rebuke, correction and reconciliation that comes along with it.

Self-examination may prevent us from being deluded, contaminated and condemned by the world. It also opens the door for the Spirit to impart spiritual gifts outlined in 1 Corinthians 12:4-11 that skillfully places Believers in various environments of engagement where those gifts will boldly advance the KOG:

"There are diversities of gifts, but the same Spirit. There are differences of ministries, but the same Lord. And there are diversities of activities, but it is the same God who works all in all. But the manifestation of the Spirit is given to each one for the profit of all: for to one is given ***the word of wisdom*** *through the Spirit, to another* ***the word of knowledge*** *through the same Spirit, to another* ***faith*** *by the same Spirit, to another* ***gifts of healings*** *by the same Spirit, to another* ***the working of miracles****, to another* ***prophecy****, to another* ***discerning of spirits****, to another* ***different kinds of tongues****, to another* ***the interpretation of tongues****. But one and the same Spirit works all these things, distributing to each one individually as He wills."*

Jesus exemplified the model for marketplace engagement with fluidity. The Apostle Paul wrote adeptly in (1 Corinthians 13:1-13) to the church at Corinth to settle the debate about the gifts one should desire. Many Corinthians desired gifts that would bring them notoriety, fame and fortune but the greatest gift we have to give is ***love.. for God is love*** (1 John 4:8):

"Though I speak with the tongues of men and of angels, but have no love, I have become sounding brass or a clanging cymbal. And though I have the gift of prophecy, and understand all mysteries and all knowledge, and though I have all faith, so that I could remove mountains, but have no love, I am nothing. And though I bestow all my goods to feed the poor, and though I give my body to be burned, but have no love, it profits me nothing.

Love suffers long and is kind; love does not envy; love does not parade itself, is not puffed up; does not behave rudely, does not seek its own, is not provoked, thinks no evil; does not rejoice in iniquity, but rejoices in the truth; bears all things, believes all things, hopes all things, endures all things.

Love never fails. But whether there are prophecies, they will fail; whether there are tongues, they will cease; whether there is knowledge, it will vanish away. For we know in part and we prophesy in part. But when that which is perfect has come, then that which is in part will be done away. When I was a child, I spoke as a child, I understood as a child, I thought as a child; but when I became a man, I put away childish things. For now we see in a mirror, dimly, but then face to face. Now I know in part, but then I shall know just as I also am known. And now abide faith, hope, love, these three; ***but the greatest of these is love."***

The conclusion of the matter is this; ***there is no crisis of spirituality in LOVE!***

Once the Believer has been equipped with the gifts, he is now ready to hit the streets! Jesus outlined His target market and plan of action for spiritual engagement in Matthew 25:33-45:

"And He will set the sheep on His right hand, but the goats on the left. Then the King will say to those on His right hand, 'Come, you blessed of My Father, inherit the kingdom prepared for you from the foundation of the world: ***for I was hungry and you gave Me food; I was thirsty and you gave Me drink; I was a stranger and you took Me in; I was naked and you clothed Me; I was sick and you visited Me; I was in prison and you came to Me.'***

"Then the righteous will answer Him, saying, 'Lord, when did we see You hungry and feed You, or thirsty and give You drink? When did we see You a stranger and take You in, or naked and clothe You? Or when did we see You sick, or in prison, and come to You?' And the King will answer and say to them, 'Assuredly, I say to you, inasmuch as you did it to one of the least of these My brethren, you did it to Me.'

“The Crisis of Spirituality”

“Then He will also say to those on the left hand, ‘Depart from Me, you cursed, into the everlasting fire prepared for the devil and his angels: for I was hungry and you gave Me no food; I was thirsty and you gave Me no drink; I was a stranger and you did not take Me in, naked and you did not clothe Me, sick and in prison and you did not visit Me.’

“Then they also will answer Him, saying, ‘Lord, when did we see You hungry or thirsty or a stranger or naked or sick or in prison, and did not minister to You?’ Then He will answer them, saying, ‘Assuredly, I say to you, inasmuch as you did not do it to one of the least of these, you did not do it to Me.”

Our inheritance for spiritual engagement and passionate devotional service in the marketplace ***is the freaking KOG!*** You have to be dead to miss that! Amen...

Chapter Four:
Functions of the Human Spirit

"Not that I have already attained, or am already perfected; but I press on, that I may lay hold of that for which Christ Jesus has also laid hold of me. Brethren, I do not count myself to have apprehended; but one thing I do, forgetting those things which are behind and reaching forward to those things which are ahead, I press toward the goal for the prize of the upward call of God in Christ Jesus. Therefore let us, as many as are mature, have this mind; and if in anything you think otherwise, God will reveal even this to you. Nevertheless, to the degree that we have already attained, let us walk by the same rule, let us be of the same mind."

(Philippians 3:12-16)

The simple message that the Apostle Paul is trying to convey is that we should not be puffed up having attained the deposit of the HS, but that we should continue to be diligent in allowing His spirit to perfect us. My perfection is Christ and my perfection is in Christ. My past is my past. I have to learn from it but I must also let it go. My sin does not define me and ***the Accuser has no power over me now that I am in Christ Jesus!***

The "upward call" mentioned here is God's requirement for righteousness, humility, submission and service. God will prune you, perfect you (through ***chastisement***) and protect you. The mindset of ***maturity*** (vv. 15) is seeded in the ***pursuit of spiritual perfection*** or passionate devotion to service in the marketplace. The HS will adjust your attitude and priorities quickly if you get offline or are unsure of which way to go!

At the end of the day, the directive is that we all have the ***same mind***; that is, the Mind of Christ, which is the Word of God.

Paul stated that once we are apprehended by God, our natural inclinations have nothing to do with how or what we are to preach and who or where we are to serve. We are charged with the responsibility to discipline those inside and outside of the faith.

Your commitment to boldly engage and empower others in the gospel of peace is predicated on the premise that you have not "arrived" (or have yet to come to the full knowledge of God). You are only a sinner saved by grace through faith in Christ Jesus not some special entity created in the heavenlies by a host of angels and are therefore totally submissive to the direction of the HS.

Three Main Functions of the Spirit

There are three main functions of the human spirit. They are the conscience, human intuition and spiritual communion.

Your ***conscience*** is an organ of discernment (reasoning). A weak mind will follow anything. It distinguishes right from wrong, not through knowledge (or the influence of) stored in the mind but by a spontaneous direct judgement:

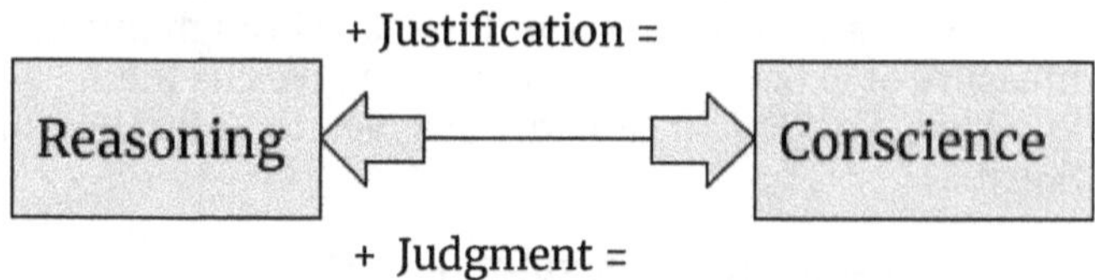

The conscience is an independent agent. It is direct and does not bend to outside opinions. Wrongdoing will raise the voice of conscience accusation in the life of a Believer. The function of conscience in a man's spirit can be found in the following scriptures: (Deuteronomy 2:30), (Psalms 34:18), (Psalms 51:10), (John 13:21), (Acts 17:16), (Romans 8:16), (2 Corinthians 2:13) and (2 Timothy 1:7).

Human **intuition** is a sensory organ and is the second function of the spirit. It is an independent entity operating outside of any external influences. Intuition comes to us without any assistance from our emotions, mental capacity or volition (will). We truly "know" something through our intuition; our mind (brain) merely helps us to understand. The revelations of God and the movements of the HS are known to us by our intuition. In order to function effectively in this realm, the Believer must heed these two elements: the voice of the conscience and the teaching of our intuition.

Communion of the spirit is fellowship (worship) with God through the power of the HS by faith and our organs of the soul (our conscience and intuition) are incompetent to worship Him. Communion creates greater God awareness. God is not apprehended by our thoughts, feelings, emotions or intentions for He can only be known in and through our spirit man:

COMMUNION + Operation in the Spirit = WORSHIP

Communion judges according to intuition. Communion condemns all conduct that does not follow the direction given by intuition. Intuition is related to communion or worship in that God is known by man intuitively and reveals His will to man through intuition. No measure of expectation or deduction gives us the knowledge of God...it can only be given to us by His Holy Spirit...

The Spirit that is NEVER in crisis!

The Crisis of Carnal Calculation

Another device that places our spirit man in crisis is our incessant desire to overthink situations. We love to sit down and calculate our circumstances. The inherent danger is that ***thought easily influences action or inaction.***

"For though we walk in the flesh, we do not war according to the flesh. For the weapons of our warfare are not carnal but mighty in God for pulling down strongholds, casting down arguments and every high thing that exalts itself against the knowledge of God, bringing every thought into captivity to the obedience of Christ,..."

(2 Corinthians 10:3-5)

CALCULATIONS = STRONGHOLDS

Our spirits are grieved when our thoughts create strongholds that erect barriers to our ability to fellowship with God through our hearts, minds and souls. The mind is held captive by the ***enemy*** *(in this case, the enemy is not the devil, but any disobedient behavior contrary to the will and word of God)* and must be freed by the HS through obedience to the WOG.

Many rebellious thoughts are housed in spiritual citadels. A ***citadel*** is a fortress usually built high on a hill surrounded by an impenetrable wall. How many of us build these walls through fear, ignorance or shame? How many strongholds are constructed through disobedience and blatant sinful behavior?

The Apostle Paul urges us to bring these thoughts and deeds into captivity. We must capture the spirit of truth and destroy the works of the enemy brick by brick until the wall has been decimated. The crisis of spirituality can be averted if we abandon the carnal mind (a mind without God) which in inherently weak and childlike:

"Therefore, since we have this ministry, as we have received mercy, we do not lose heart. But we have renounced the hidden things of shame, not walking in craftiness nor

handling the word of God deceitfully, but by manifestation of the truth commending ourselves to every man's conscience in the sight of God. But even if our gospel is veiled, ***it is veiled to those who are perishing, whose minds the god of this age has blinded,*** *who do not believe, lest the light of the gospel of the glory of Christ, who is the image of God, should shine on them." (2 Corinthians 4:4)*

The mind that is set on the flesh is hostile to God (2 Cor. 3:14), (Ephesians 2:3) and (Romans 8:7). The genesis of the mind is the stronghold of the enemy at the beginning. This ***"infiltration"*** is innate and germinates out of control in the sinner's life eventually overtaking the will, emotion and spirit thus completing this evil cycle of delusion.

Presentation is what avails itself to the eyes at the onset. In other words, it is what is presented to the subject as ***bait*** (the enemy serves up the thing that we love the most: porn, drugs, illicit sex, thuggery, etc.). The mind is the infiltration point and it is the place where the spirit in crisis agrees with the sinful act. This action is also referred to as ***temptation.***

The flesh (sinful behavior) is then used to secure the consent of the body and mind in this equation. I always say, ***"The FLESH never forgets!"*** Temptation (sin) and thoughts are inseparable unless crucified daily. Our intellect (reasoning) obstructs our ability to apprehend the Spirit of God. Contrition leads to repentance (Acts 11:18). Repentance disrupts the chaos and creates a significant breach in the mind's stronghold. This significant breach is called ***peace*** which elicits a new mind. When you receive a new mind (peace) you will receive a new heart and a new spirit aligned with the cosmos or universal order of the original intent of God.

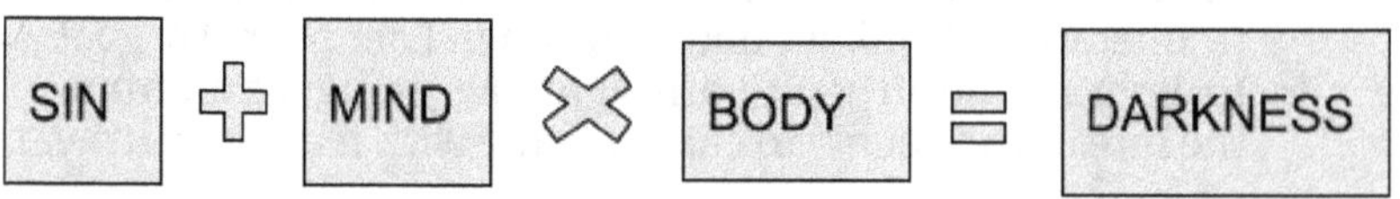

Knowing Him Through the Spirit

"...that I may know Him and the power of His resurrection, and the fellowship of His sufferings, being conformed to His death..."

(Philippians 3:10)

The goal of the spiritual saint is not to ***"realize"*** (know himself) but, rather to ***<u>know</u>*** Jesus Christ. The saint must secure the realization of Jesus Christ in all things great and small. In ***Christian work*** (passionate devotional service in the marketplace), I have come to realize that something has to be done and that I must do it. I also realize that I cannot do it alone and that the HS has whispered life changing assignments into the ears of dozens of others who have accepted the call to ***"worship"*** (serving God's people in the marketplace).

Worship is the confirmation of the individual's ***death in Christ***. That is, dying to oneself for the sake of boldly advancing the KOG; first, in the spiritual realm and then in the natural realm. In death, it is the Spirit that affords me the opportunity to be the ***resurrection*** in Christ through submission to the will of God and by conforming to His death (or worship) as I gave away all ***worldly things*** (that is, ***premeditated*** sinful behavior) and counted them as loss so that I could gain Christ.

This perspective is accentuated in as much as the recognition of Jesus Christ as the prime directive should be continual as we strive to walk out God's mandate (will) for our lives. I will not love God anymore when I am rich (monetarily). I will not hate Him when I am poor. My goal is to embrace the struggle with righteous indignation from the lure of the enemy to captivate me with fear and betrayal.

As I am enduring the suffering, I will fully realize the power of His resurrection and, more importantly, His death. As a saint, I have the ***privilege of suffering with Christ*** and it is this suffering that qualifies me for sonship and a right to all the benefits of the KOG as a citizen, servant and friend of the King to the glory of God. Amen.

"The righteous cry out, and the Lord hears, and delivers them out of all their troubles. The Lord is near to those who have a broken heart, and saves such as have a ***contrite spirit.*** *Many are the afflictions of the righteous, but the Lord delivers him out of them all. He guards all his bones; not one of them is broken."*

(Psalms 34:17-20)

The Spirit and Ministry of Persecution

"But you have carefully followed my doctrine, manner of life, purpose, faith, longsuffering, love, perseverance, persecutions, afflictions, which happened to me at Antioch, at Iconium, at Lystra—what persecutions I endured. And out of them all the Lord delivered me. Yes, and all who desire to live godly in Christ Jesus will suffer persecution."

(2 Timothy 3:11-12)

In this scripture, the Apostle Paul is exhorting his disciple Timothy to wrap his mind around the fact that he is going to suffer persecution for carrying the banner of Christ Jesus. I am sure Timothy was sweating bullets as Paul recapped his life of persecution in great detail so as to prepare the young man for the arduous physical and spiritual journey ahead.

Like most everything else, persecution is a spirit and a ministry. Faith in the Spirit compels the one being persecuted to endure because the God of Abraham, Isaac and Jabob will deliver you. And, even if He doesn't deliver you, ***He is able!*** The crisis in spirituality associated with persecution is having the willingness to suffer and the fortitude to endure.

Persecution can be summarized by conducting a comparative analysis of the anatomy of death or dying to oneself. "***Personal execution***" or persecution represents the cutting away of ***strongholds*** (fortresses or bunkers) in your life. We will most certainly build an impenetrable wall or dig our heels in within a nanosecond to defend our position on a matter we feel strongly about. The HS showed me a long time ago that ***people will believe what they want to believe no matter how compelling the evidence (truth) may be to the contrary!***

Persecution establishes a covenant with God. It is not important to defend yourself; however, it is more important to defend the God in you by resisting the evil thoughts that come upon you. The goal of the Believer is ***spiritual integrity*** with regard to sacrificing oneself for the Gospel of Peace as Jesus did for us. The destruction of His flesh allowed us to experience His mortality (His ability and willingness to suffer persecution) void of His works which did not save Him.

But what did save Him and all Believers was His ***obedience (submission) to death.*** The beautiful revelation of our death versus the death of Christ is that our death is a ***"living death."*** Just think about that for a moment. Jesus actually died on the Cross and had to be resurrected by His Father. True Believers get the benefit of a transformative life without physically dying! Now that is something to shout about! You can boldly declare, *"Here I am*" and then confidently move forward to serve the people God has given to you (Hebrews 2:13).

In this instance submission equates to "service"and is identified as the true source of His power in death. Christ as the Messiah gives us a vivid picture of the ministry of persecution. It is not how many times you suffer or how long you suffer. The details of your ordeal are irrelevant, the character of the perpetrator against you is not a factor and your economic status or educational pedigree mean absolutely nothing. All that matters is your ***posture or spiritual compass (where you are spiritually in relationship to God).*** Am I lost at sea or am I on course to inherit the KOG? Is your confidence in the ***"breakthrough"*** or in Jesus Christ?

Will you persevere until you receive the gift of transformation from the suffering and persecuted slave to the passionately devoted servant and friend of the King of Glory? Selah...

The Spirit of Disobedience

"Let no one deceive you with empty words, for because of these things the wrath of God comes upon the sons of disobedience."

(Ephesians 5:6)

In the spiritual world there is a hierarchy of demons directly assigned to idols (idolatry) and sin. These sins include pride, envy, greed, sloth, lust, anger and gluttony. The demonic angels assigned to these spirits have names: Lucifer (pride), Asmodeus (lust), Satan (anger), Beelzebub (gluttony), Belphegor (sloth), Mammon (greed) and Leviathan (envy) and they all have a directive to keep the immature Christian bound in fear so that they can steal his faith!

The prevalence of sin is the result of disobedience!

To meet any need through dishonesty or trickery is lust. Lust is a sin and sin equates to disobedience of God's Word. Disobedience opens the unsuspecting Christian to emotional wounds and *"**seducing spirits.**"* These spirits can be either subtle or profound; many times the individual experiences both.

These seducing spirits include, but are not limited to:

- ***rebellion**: witchcraft and sorcery, both literally and figuratively (i.e. manipulation of a weaker vessel through influence, fear and/or intimidation to get them to do your will).*
- *carnal state of mind or **carnality**: these spirits place their victims under siege at night even while they sleep with perverted thoughts, images and suggestions;*
- ***unforgiveness**: this is a very destructive and dangerous spirit because the spirit of unforgiveness cuts the individual off directly from fellowship with God;*
- ***bitterness**: stifles the grace of God and His protection; it gives access to every demon in hell to invade your **temple** (physical body, mind, soul and spirit).*

As you grow in faith and break the shackles of bondage to fear in order to navigate safely through the waters of the spirit realm, you will have to have the Holy Spirit leading and guiding your every step. These demons work in concert with your "deception" and wicked heart to manipulate and distort your present realities. The Lord God is your "present" help in your time of need.

Don't allow the calamities of life to drive a wedge between you and the Lord. Much of the adversity we encounter in our lives is a direct result of our unrighteous choices; not God punishing us. God didn't hand you the crack pipe, place you on the street corner to deal drugs or hold a gun to your head to get you to rob that bank! It was you or the people in your sphere of influence. Be wise about the company you keep and whom you call "friend."

Demons know exactly what you like and they have keen insight into the heart of mankind and possess the ability to manufacture ***any*** IDOL you want to worship...anytime, any place. Selah.

The Spirit of Separation

"For He Himself is our peace, who has made both one, and has broken down the middle wall of ***separation****, having abolished in His flesh the enmity, that is, the law of commandments contained in ordinances, so as to create in Himself one new man from the two, thus making peace, and that He might reconcile them both to God in one body through the cross, thereby putting to death the enmity. And He came and preached peace to you who were far off and to those who were near. For through Him we both have access by one Spirit to the Father."*

(Ephesians 2:14-18)

There was an actual wall (partition) erected in the temple area separating the Jews and the Gentiles with a sign posted warning that any Gentiles going beyond the Court of the Gentiles would receive swift and sudden death. This separation was a stark reaction to paganism and the bleak condition they faced in ancient Israel. However, they had hope and didn't even know it in that Jesus went to the Cross and died for them so that their unrighteousness and inability to follow the Law would be "handled" by the Resurrected Christ.

Christ was the bridge that aborted the separation between those wallowing on the other side in darkness clamoring for a better way to live and those seeking peace, love and joy. Christ is the peace of all Believers and Satan represents the crisis in spirituality for all those living in the shadows of the Light (Christ).

A potter sits at his wheel and plops down a mound of clay without form. He sits there for a while fashioning his creation in his mind. He sees something in the lump of clay. What does he see? What statement does he want to make with his piece or does he just want to make something beautiful? So begins the process...the clay (sinful man) is transformed into God's ***workmanship,*** ("***poiema***" in Greek, #4161; Strong's Concordance) literally, "a thing made." It is translated into English as the word ***"poem."*** The word intimates a handiwork or masterpiece created in Christ Jesus for good works that God predestined for Believers from the foundation of the world (Ephesians 2:4-10).

The whole idea behind the spirit of separation is to keep someone away from somebody or something. It implies division. Specifically, it is the ultimate goal of the enemy to keep the person in darkness away from exposure to the light of the gospel of peace. But in the KOG, separation is a ***"seed."*** It represents a new beginning, a pivotal change in the spiritual life of one thirsty for the love of God. The seed of separation fosters growth and development and challenges the new Believer to stay on course in his pursuit of righteousness.

A pearl is formed when one grain of sand separates itself from the rest and agitates the membrane of an oyster. The pearl is a magnificent creation as a direct result of the introduction of an irritant (sand, food) in which the mollusk secretes ***nacre*** (mother of pearl) to protect itself from the invasion. The organic material covers the particle with multiple layers as a defense mechanism. And so, a pearl is formed. In this case, separation is good.

The other night, I was speaking to my wife Olivia about how separation can impact a marriage. My contention is that if two people decide to separate in order to heal their marriage, they are creating a ***placebo effect*** (false sense of progress with an inert subject) for an illness that requires ***authentic medicine*** (effective communication that builds and maintains trust). It has been my experience that the overwhelming majority of couples that make the decision to separate have no intention of repairing the breach.

They covet the ***"freedom of darkness"***(the ability to move about with no accountability) versus the "freedom of the light" (the hard work required to cultivate and maintain strong relationships). In my opinion, when a married couple agrees to separate, what they are really saying in the spirit is, "I quit!" You cannot restore something as important as a marriage from a distance. ***The deception in separation/divorce is freedom.*** The reality in most cases is ***misery*** (alimony, child support, fractured relationships) and a great sense of loss. Something (faith, hope) is dead once you separate and the prevailing spiritual crisis is that there is no peace (the ability to rest in Christ). Amen.

Spiritual Witness Protection

"He who dwells in the secret place of the Most High Shall abide under the shadow of the Almighty." (Psalm 91:1)

"How precious is Your loving kindness, O God! Therefore the children of men put their trust under the shadow of Your wings." (Psalm 36:7)

"Keep me as the apple of Your eye; Hide me under the shadow of Your wings...," (Psalm 17:8)

The WOG clearly states that the safest place for any person is under the shadow of the Almighty (in His Presence). These three scriptures accentuate the power of intimacy, love and reverential fear of the Lord. His Presence occupies every square inch of all creation; there is no place you can go beyond His reach and protection. Conversely, there is also no place you can hide from His chastisement, punishment or correction.

The elements of ***carnal witness protection*** are centered around someone committing a crime, some government agency or branch of law enforcement not being able to catch the ringleader of the criminal organization and then finally, after an exhaustive investigation, apprehending an associate of the primary suspect they hope to "flip" and help them catch the Big Boss.

The "snitch" or "rat" is offered immunity from any type of punishment, a brand new identity, relocation to some obscure place far away, protection and finances (job, housing, car, etc.). In the end, the person appears to be free but, in reality, is captive to his own fear and paranoia as he will never be at peace while "looking over his shoulder" the rest of his life hoping that his past will never catch up with him. The witness is, in effect, anonymous.

Conversely, in the KOG as a witness for the King of Glory you are utterly protected. Even the ***witness*** (testimony, evidence) of the ***witness*** (the individual experiencing the metamorphosis) is protected! How strong is that? When your words echo His words, you can't miss; the words will rest softly upon the heart or shake the foundation of the life of the person. The HS will do whatever it takes to get them to deafen their ears to the voice of the enemy.

"You are My witnesses," says the Lord, "And My servant whom I have chosen, that you may know and believe Me, and understand that I am He. Before Me there was no God formed, nor shall there be after Me. (Isaiah 43:10)"

A witness for the Lord, is bold and assertive as he seeks out the lost and broken. He is not in exile under an assumed name or hiding in plain sight. His time in ***isolation*** has prepared him for the fire and he is willing and able to enter into the KOD with the hedge of protection and leading of the HS. Christ's command to be His witnesses is given to all Believers to spread the gospel of the KOG regardless of the consequences. The power in the testimony or witness is not in attempting to *"convince"* people of the virtue of the WOG, but to display its power in the reality of the transformed life that you are walking in. All Believers have a formidable weapon in their arsenals; the indwelling of the Holy Spirit. The HS is the ***"dunamis"*** or explosive, dynamic power given to us by God to resist the wiles of the enemy and destroy the works of the devil. Amen.

Chapter Five:
The Crisis of Spiritual Reproduction

"For the ***word of God*** *is living and powerful, and sharper than any two-edged sword, piercing even to the division of soul and spirit, and of joints and marrow, and is a discerner of the thoughts and intents of the heart."*

(Hebrews 4:12)

The mindset of the Believer is being pushed by the HS into the spirit of reproducing Christ in the earth. God thinks generationally; what most Christians don't or won't do because they are stuck drinking the ***religious serum (milk)*** produced by barren church leaders that have no motivation for passionate devotional service.

God works through generations and through seasons. God's most powerful tools to ***reproduce Christ*** in the earth are His Word and His Spirit. The Gospel of John 1:1-14 (Amplified version) delineates this point with perfection:

"In the beginning [before all time] was the Word (Christ), and the Word was with God, and the Word was God Himself. He was [continually existing] in the beginning [co-eternally] with God. All things were made and came into existence through Him; ***and without Him not even one thing was made that has come into being.*** *In Him was life [and the power to bestow life], and life was the Light of men. The Light shines on in the darkness, and the darkness did not understand it or overpower it or appropriate it or absorb it [and is unreceptive to it].*

There came a man commissioned and sent from God, whose name was John. This man came as a witness, to testify about the Light, so that all might believe [in Christ, the Light] through him. John was not the Light, but came to testify about the Light. There it was—the true Light [the genuine, perfect, steadfast Light] which, coming into the world, enlightens everyone. He (Christ) was in the world, and though the world was made through Him, the world did not recognize Him. He came to that which was His own [that which belonged to Him—His world, His creation, His possession], and those who were His own [people—the Jewish nation] did not receive and welcome Him. But to as many as did receive and welcome Him, He gave the right [the authority, the privilege] to become children of God, that is, to those who believe in (adhere to, trust in, and rely on) His name—who were born, not of blood [natural conception], nor of the will of the flesh [physical impulse], nor of the will of man [that of a natural father], but of God [that is, a divine and supernatural birth—they are born of God—spiritually transformed, renewed, sanctified].

And the Word (Christ) became flesh, and lived among us; and we [actually] saw His glory, glory as belongs to the [One and] only begotten Son of the Father, [the Son who is truly unique, the only One of His kind, who is] full of grace and truth (absolutely free of deception)."

This is one of my favorite scriptures in the Bible because it illustrates the power of the ***spirit of recognition*** displayed by John the Baptist. John knew why he was sent to set the table for Jesus and that his role was important. John was the bulldozer, the earthmover and the ox that pulled the plough. He was called to make the crooked paths straight for Christ. John was a seed and planted seeds for His predecessor and followers. Wait a minute. How can someone come (be produced or created) before you and after you? John said this about Jesus (John 1:30). This is the amazing potency of spiritual reproduction; the Word is truly a living organism.

The Word *(Greek-**"ho logos"**)* was utilized to illuminate the principle of the universe, especially the creative energy that fashioned the entire universe. Perhaps Logos has some connection with the OT presentation of Wisdom as an embodiment or attribute of God (Proverbs 8). In both the Jewish conception and the Greek, the Logos has been identified with the idea of a genesis; specifically, the framing of the worlds through the mouth of God (Genesis 1:3). Logos is the personification of God's Truth and

Wisdom and the cosmic Mediator between Yahweh and all creation that reveals Christ as the Incarnation of the Word.

The Word exemplifies the purest form and ***definition of faith.*** Christ communicated this thought in its simplicity by saying to the ruler of the synagogue whose daughter had just died, *"Do not be afraid;* ***only believe****"(Mark 5:36).*

Reproducing Wheat Amongst the Tares

"...but while men slept, his enemy came and ***sowed tares among the wheat*** *and went his way." (Matthew 13:25)*

I am a huge fan of music. I listen to many different genres; country, rock, reggae, classical, funk, R&B and jazz. But what really brings me joy and happiness is hearing the music from the 60's and 70's; the ***love*** generation. All of the songs were about love and marriage and family. That generation produced the men and women God would call to sow love, peace and joy into the earth. This is the ***wheat. And then we fell asleep.***

The current generation has created a brand of music whose trademark is centered on ***lust*** not love. I know this generation absolutely worships this music but its misogynistic, degrading and profane content has no appeal to me at all. They are the ***tares.***

Normally the tares (KOD) are sown among the wheat (KOG) because they are similar in composition, structure and appearance. The primary difference between the two is that the tares labor in secrecy underground to destroy the roots (foundation) of the wheat with the destruction being undetectable to the naked eye. That's the way the KID aborts the reproduction of the spirit in the earth realm; through the mechanism of ***subliminal seduction.***

The Body of Christ (BOC) fell asleep. It got lazy and puffed up and self-centered. It became focused on the needs of men versus the will of God. It became hostile toward holiness, righteousness and goodness. It became the bastard instead of the son and it abandoned the halls of justice and peace for the confines of spiritual brothels and whoredom. In the process, the modern day church has produced an entire generation of ***spiritual eunuchs.*** This is a spiritual crisis of mammoth proportions!

I would estimate that right around the time of the late 1950's until the late 1960's, God used our mothers and fathers (***drunkards in the spirit*** because they did not actively pursue the things of God) to sneak us into the earth realm as wheat to be sown among the tares (our parents' and grandparents' generation). Many of them were stuck in worldly mindsets and religiosity. Although I must admit the grandparents did try to lay a solid foundation of family rooted and grounded in the institution of marriage. Our generation had melodies of love in our hearts and minds. Not so for the tares.

The tares have a musical influence predicated on lust, sex and a mutual lack of commitment. They could care less about building strong families or fatherhood and certainly not marriage. These children born in the 1980's and 1990's have become the Great Apostasy; they have fallen away from the love of God. The entire generation has not abandoned reproduction, but they have abandoned ***reproducing Christ.*** They have, however, created a new generation of **bastards** (children who don't know their spiritual Father). This generation of tares have melodies of lust in their hearts and minds. The prophet Haggai boldly states in (Haggai 1:3-7):

*"Then the word of the Lord came by Haggai the prophet, saying, "Is it time for you yourselves to dwell in your paneled houses, and this temple to lie in ruins?" Now therefore, thus says the Lord of hosts: **"Consider your ways!***

"You have sown much, and bring in little; You eat, but do not have enough; You drink, but you are not filled with drink; You clothe yourselves, but no one is warm; And he who earns wages, Earns wages to put into a bag with holes."

Thus says the Lord of hosts: ***"Consider your ways!"***

Haggai was basically saying to the current generation of young people, "What in the hell are yall doin'? Wake up!" Almighty God does not waste His time speaking to a crowd of people. He desires and prefers intimacy without distraction from the cares of your life. So why are you trying to get close to God sittin' in a church building? If you want to get tight with the HS, go to the mountains, get the stuff you need and come back down and build Him a temple (your mortal body) He can dwell in to glorify the Father (1 Corinthians 6:19).

Reproduction does not require any special skills or attributes; a sperm and an egg are gonna do what they do without your help! But spiritual reproduction requires time, love and intimacy. You will also suffer and experience trouble and tribulation. The underlying paradox in the KOG is that loss in the world equates to gain in the KOG and gain in the world equates to loss in the KOG. Reproducing Christ encompasses absolute freedom for the Believer and a guarantee of ***safety*** (the promise of eternal life in His Presence).

It signifies a ***living resurrection*** and new birth; in other words, a veritable partnership with the Lamb of God to boldly advance the KOG and to secure our citizenship in heaven. The wheat will dwell with the Father and the tares will be thrown into the fire to be consumed for eternity. Paul seals this truth with his revelation in (Philippians 3:7-11):

"*But what things were gained to me, these I have counted loss for Christ. Yet indeed I also count all things loss for the excellence of the knowledge of Christ Jesus my Lord, for whom I have suffered the loss of all things, and count them as rubbish,* ***<u>that I may gain Christ and be found in Him</u>****, not having my own righteousness, which is from the law, but that which is through faith in Christ, the righteousness which is from God by faith; that I may know Him and the power of His resurrection, and the fellowship of His sufferings, being* *conformed to His death, if, by any means, I may attain to the resurrection from the dead."*

The Spirit of Wisdom

"Therefore I also, after I heard of your faith in the Lord Jesus and your love for all the saints, do not cease to give thanks for you, making mention of you in my prayers: that the God of our Lord Jesus Christ, the Father of glory, may give to you ***the spirit of wisdom*** *and revelation in the knowledge of Him, the eyes of your understanding being enlightened; that you may know what is the hope of His calling, what are the riches of the glory of His inheritance in the saints, and what is the exceeding greatness of His power toward us who believe, according to the working of His mighty power which He worked in Christ when He raised Him from the dead and seated Him at His right hand in the heavenly places, far above all principality and power and might and dominion, and every name that is named, not only in this age but also in that which is to come.*

And He put all things under His feet, and gave Him to be head over all things to the church, which is His body, the fullness of Him who fills all in all."

(Ephesians 1:15-23)

Spiritual wisdom is the cornerstone of maturity in the life of the Believer that affords him the desire and ability to duplicate Christ in the earth. Wisdom is the receptacle of revelation from the HS; a reservoir of His Holy Word. Through spiritual wisdom we fully understand the Preeminence of Christ (Colossians 1:9-18) and have the confidence to execute His plan for salvation in the marketplace.

Spiritual wisdom is transferable but it comes at a cost (suffering). After the Believer has endured his trials and tribulations, he will become a stout ambassador for the KOG. To what end you might ask? The apostle Paul answers this question with precision in (Colossians 1:24-29):

*"I now rejoice in my **sufferings** for you, and fill up in my flesh what is lacking in the afflictions of Christ, for the sake of His body, which is the church, of which I became a minister according to the **stewardship** from God which was given to me for you, to **fulfill the word of God**, the **mystery** which has been hidden from ages and from generations, but now has been revealed to His saints. To them God willed to make known what are the riches of the glory of this mystery among the Gentiles: which is **Christ in you, the hope of glory**. Him we **preach, warning every man** and teaching every man in all wisdom, that we may present every man perfect in Christ Jesus. To this end I also labor, striving according to **His working** which works in me mightily."*

In the Book of Ephesians, Paul professes the guarantee of our inheritance which is the HS Himself. As a matter of fact, the Greek word for ***guarantee*** can also be used to indicate an ***engagement ring***. As Christ is the Bridegroom and the BOC is the bride, the expectation is that when the marriage is consummated, the result will be a spiritual birth or spiritual reproduction. The seal or mark in the life of a Believer is the Presence of the HS manifested in His will to fellowship with His sons throughout eternity.

The spiritual wisdom we extract from this revelation is that there is purpose (*prosthesis*, Greek) and counsel (*boule*, Greek) in the will (*thelema*, Greek) of God. God's purpose conveys the idea of desire, even a heart's desire, for the word primarily expresses ***emotion*** instead of volition. Therefore God's will is not so much God's ***intention***, as it is His ***heart's desire***. The word prosthesis denotes an intention or a plan; it literally means a "blueprint." This plan was created in God's counsel, the result of ***deliberate determination*** from a Mastermind with a heart of love.

The conclusion of the matter is this, I cannot fail as long as I strive to imitate and duplicate Christ Jesus in the marketplace. Selah...

The Spirit of Isolation

*"A man who **isolates** himself seeks his own desire; He rages against all wise judgment."*
(Proverbs 18:1)

There is a profound difference between a man that isolates himself and a man God chooses to isolate. The spirit of isolation and the crucible of loneliness is where the ***anointing (the yoke destroying, burden removing power of God)*** is tempered and molded and shaped and fashioned into a ***ministry*** that will be able to withstand the powers of the enemy as you boldly advance the KOG. If you are going to do a great thing publicly, you will have to do a great thing privately with God.

When a man isolates himself, it is usually a result of a series of traumatic experiences; lifelong ridicule, death of a loved one, Daddy or Mommy issues, being rejected by a lover or the loss of a job they have held for a long time.

In the place of isolation with the HS you will undergo a ***spiritual metamorphosis*** (*'meta morpho'* in Greek) or transfiguration. In short, you will see the Resurrected Christ and lay down your 2000 year old Jesus hanging on the Cross at Calvary.

There are three things you will experience while in isolation with the HS: ***convergence, caution and clarity.*** With ***convergence***, you will be faced with a focalizing or *confluence* (point of intersection) where various things crystallize from different directions. All the disjointed pieces (the things you weren't sure about) will be put together and clarified by the HS. In Matthew 17:1-13, Jesus is transfigured before Peter, James and John on Mount Hermon rising about 9,400 feet above sea level. Once at the top of the mountain, Jesus revealed His absolute deity to the three men. Their natural eyesight was replaced with supernatural vision enabling them to see the vision of Elijah and Moses.

Moses represented the Law and Elijah represented the prophets or prophetic utterance from God through their mouths. Together they represented the convergence of the past and the future. In other words, that which has been established and that which will be established. The vision symbolized ***hindsight*** meeting ***foresigh***t while giving the three men ***insight***.

They heard the voice of God as He spoke to them confirming once again the triune Spirit of Jesus as the Son of the Living God. In isolation together separated from the twelve, the three apostles experienced the anointing as they worshipped God in His Presence. They also felt His ***"touch"*** that gave them clarity and focus and a clear understanding that although the elders had a significant role in the movement, nothing they did was more significant than what Jesus was about to do on the Cross and none of them had a more important relationship with God than the Son of Man. The touch of the Lord has been unprecedented throughout the WOG. The ***touch*** also denoted that in the end Jesus would stand alone as the Savior of mankind and that no other man would be ***beloved of God*** thus solidifying His spiritual position as ***Jehovah Raph***a (The Lord that Heals) (Matthew 8:3, 17:7, 20:34; Mark 5:27, 30; Luke 8:45-46, 22:51).

It is vital for all Believers to both know and understand their spiritual position. At this point of revelation, you must proceed with ***caution.*** Once the HS gives us revelation as to where we are positioned spiritually in relation to Christ, we must then do what we ***know*** God wants us to do, rather than doing what we ***think*** God wants us to do. This is one of the postulates of avoiding a spiritual crisis.

Finally, while in isolation with the King of Glory, you will experience ***clarity*** (Habakkuk 2:2). Success in the KOG will be contingent upon your ability to adapt to the changes God sets in your path in real time. Don't be surprised when the course of your life's direction is altered. God will have you going one way today and then another way tomorrow. Don't be concerned about what you told people yesterday and what direction God had you going. As long as the message is clear to you, that is all that matters.

Isolation creates a dispensation in time for the Believer to fellowship with the Creator while exploiting his nakedness and all of his vulnerabilities. It is crucial to lay it on the line so that the Father can perform surgery on your heart, mind, body and soul. The ***"spiritual ICU"*** in the Presence of God with the help of the HS is the best place for repentance, redemption and reconciliation to receive fresh revelation from the throne room of Grace.

Chapter Six:
Earth's Crisis and the Spirit of Noah

"Now it came to pass, when men began to multiply on the face of the earth, and daughters were born to them, that the sons of God saw the daughters of men, that they were beautiful; and they took wives for themselves of all whom they chose. And the Lord said, "My Spirit shall not strive with man forever, for he is indeed flesh; yet his days shall be one hundred and twenty years." There were giants on the earth in those days, and also afterward, when the sons of God came into the daughters of men and they bore children to them. Those were the mighty men who were of old, men of renown.

Then the Lord saw that the wickedness of man was great in the earth, and that every intent of the thoughts of his heart was only evil continually. And the Lord was sorry that He had made man on the earth, and He was grieved in His heart. So the Lord said, "I will destroy man whom I have created from the face of the earth, both man and beast, creeping thing and birds of the air, for I am sorry that I have made them." ***But Noah found grace in the eyes of the Lord."***

(Genesis 6:1-8)

Man was not born corrupt, but mankind corrupted itself through the ***lust of the flesh, the lust of the eyes and the pride of life*** *(1 John 2:16)*. The crisis that inhabited the earth was instigated by free will and corroborated by the three spirits mentioned above. Man's eyes have always gotten him in trouble. Man's heart exacerbated the dilemma. Man's mind and spirit were continually focused on evil to the point where God was sorry He had created us.

When a man sees something, he's gotta have it...no matter what the cost! And sadly, remorse only precedes repentance when the individual gets caught in sin or suffers a staggering loss of some sort. Other than that, the spirit of remorse and the spirit of repentance are not a part of the equation and the sinner proceeds to plan his next caper.

The name Noah means ***"rest or comfort"*** in Hebrew. The spirit of Noah represents the declaration or ***kerygmatic*** *(the proclamation of religious truths, especially as taught in the Gospels)* profession of virtue. God saw that Noah's life was laced with integrity and goodness and knew that he would be faithful to fulfill his assignment to build the ark.

God was filled with wrath and committed to destroy the earth and everything in it. Noah closed the door on everybody he knew with the exception of his household (family). The door was closed because people did not understand what Noah was saying because there was no point of reference in the vernacular of that day. He had been ridiculed for his faithfulness in building the ark and his prophetic utterances of rain that would destroy the earth. So, in a spiritual sense, ***Noah represents closing the door on those who don't believe.***

The spirit of Noah eradicates the spirit of slothfulness, greed, envy, gluttony, pride, wrath and lust (the results of disobedience to the Word of God). Noah is a place of spiritual rest, comfort and peace (Psalm 91:1). Although Noah was a person, Noah is a living spirit and a destination for every Believer.

God usurps time to bring together men who are committed to boldly advancing the KOG and who believe in Him. It is the confluence of two of the most profound (and perhaps least discussed) principles in the KOG: ***quantum mechanics*** (QM)and ***proprietary knowledge*** (PK). QM is a mathematical equation of reality that is diametrically opposed to common sense (or the precepts of ***faith***). It is not the failings of QM but of mankind's inability to understand the intricacies of space and time (or the concepts associated with ***eternity***). QM refers to a discrete assignment of quantum theory to certain physical quantities such as the energy of an atom at rest.

QM and PK have a symbiotic relationship and were manifested in eternity as God created the worlds with His Word. QM is a fusion of space and time and PK is how everything works together for the good and the inherent knowledge of all things in creation. PK is how a pine tree knows how and when to germinate, the gestation period and the appropriate time to release the pine needles to the ground. The width of the trunk, the type of fruit, its color, size and taste are all coded in its DNA; its height and weight are all predetermined in eternity and manifests in time through a seed:

"Beware of false prophets, who come to you in sheep's clothing, but inwardly they are ravenous wolves. You will know them by their fruits. Do men gather grapes from thornbushes or figs from thistles? Even so, every good tree bears good fruit, but a bad tree bears bad fruit. A good tree cannot bear bad fruit, nor can a bad tree bear good fruit. Every tree that does not bear good fruit is cut down and thrown into the fire. Therefore by their fruits you will know them." (Mark 7:15-20)

PK resides within the heart and mind of God. It is the seat of omnipotence, omniscience and omnipresence. PK is literally God's ***exclusive ownership*** of all wisdom and knowledge that is disseminated to His sons in the faith by the HS. PK is given to us on a "need to know" basis. A perfect example of PK is the instruction given to Noah to build the ark. I am sure Noah thought to himself, *"What the heck is an ark?"* The rest, they say, is history!

Many of the things that man throws away in his spiritual walk become building blocks for his ***spiritual citadel***. Ridicule, shame and alienation for Noah became his righteous foundation. Patience and submission were his brick and mortar. PK underscores the mandate of belief (Mark 9:23), is the bedrock of our faith and is ***transferable***. The fact that we are *"doing something"* (conducting community outreach programs) doesn't mean that we are successful in serving. The litmus test for success can only be measured by the virtuous transformation of a person's spirit that tangibly reproduces Christ in the earth (John 15:5, 16).

The Spirit of the Promised Land

"Now this is the commandment, and these are the statutes and judgments which the Lord your God has commanded to teach you, that you may observe them in the land which you are crossing over to possess, that you may fear the Lord your God, to keep all His statutes and His commandments which I command ***you, you and your son and your grandson, all the days of your life****, and that your days may be prolonged. Therefore hear, O Israel, and be careful to observe it, that it may be well with you, and that you may multiply greatly as the Lord God of your fathers has promised you—'a land flowing with milk and honey."*

(Deuteronomy 6:1-3)

God had one simple rule, *"Obey Me and keep My laws."* The reward for the Believer would be a long life, receipt of His ***increase*** (wisdom, authority and rank in the KOG) and ***peace, love and joy in the HS.*** This is the spirit of the Promised Land: peace, love and joy. Any day that you are blessed to wake up, if your love, peace or joy is out of whack; you have just taken one step outside of the KOG.

When this occurs, your spirit man will be grieved. It will require your immediate attention to correct the problem. In the Book of Numbers, the spies were dispatched to seek out the land promised to them by the God of Abraham, Isaac and Jacob. The twelve men were tasked with gathering intelligence on the Land of Canaan and they were to report their findings back to Moses.

In retrospect, this should have been an easy gig because the Lord God had already given the land to them. He just wanted them to see the abundance and bring back the praise report to lift the countenance of the congregation. But things went sideways quickly when the spies saw the sons of Anak (giants in the land measuring 7 to 9 feet tall) roaming about and realized that in order to enter into the land they had to utterly destroy the giants!

After 40 days, they returned to Moses and Aaron and gave them a bad report, *"Then Caleb quieted the people before Moses, and said,* ***"Let us go up at once and take possession, for we are well able to overcome it."*** *But the men who had gone up with him said, "We are not able to go up against the people, for they are stronger than us." And they gave the children of Israel a bad report of the land which they had spied out, saying, "The land through which we have gone as spies is a land that devours its inhabitants, and all the people whom we saw in it are men of great stature. There we saw the giants (the descendants of Anak came from the giants); and* ***we were like grasshoppers in our own sight, and so we were in their sight."*** *(Numbers 13:30-33)*

Only Joshua and Caleb believed the words of the Lord. They witnessed the hand of Almighty God sustaining them for 40 years in the Wilderness and they knew they were going to win with the help of the Lord. Caleb was 40 years old at the time of the mission, so he had spent his entire life in the desert. I am sure he was ready to do whatever was necessary to get the heck out of there. The congregation was so mad with Calab and Joshua that they wanted to stone them for bringing back the report that they should move ahead with plans to fight the giants.

The other ten spies were smitten with leprosy and death as were all their generations above the age of 20 years. The Lord God also promised that they would never enter into the Promised Land so He declared that the carcasses of the ***"evil congregation"*** would rot in the wilderness and their children would reap the benefits of the land flowing with milk and honey. The reference to ***"grasshoppers"*** is the Hebrew word ***"chagab"*** *(Strong's #2284)* which is a simile for ***insignificance.***

This is the spirit that kindled the wrath of God. He told them who they were in His sight and what He had already done and promised what He was going to do and they still didn't believe Him! He had a 100% execution rate on His Promises and He had grown weary of their folly and rejection. This crisis in spirituality is still prevalent today. God tells us something positive and good, but people want to believe the enemy and his negativity and dim the life in the hearts of the brethren because of fear and doubt.

The spirit of fear among leadership is transferable just as the spirit of faith is ruthless in the face of danger and opposition. Whose report will you believe? Selah...

The Spirit of the Fathers

"Behold, I will send you Elijah the prophet. Before the coming of the great and dreadful day of the Lord. And he will turn The hearts of the fathers to the children, And the hearts of the children to their fathers, Lest I come and strike the earth with a curse."

(Malachi 4:5-6)

God thinks and works generationally. It has always been God's intention (the desire of His heart) that the hearts of the fathers be turned towards the hearts of their children and their children's children. The ***spiritual crisis in the earth today*** is that the hearts of the fathers are not turned toward their sons and daughters.

I come from three generations of forefathers whose hearts were made of stone (Ezekiel 36:26). It was God's heart's desire that the father's would love their sons and daughters, but there have been generations of bastards born to bastards. A bastard seed will produce a bastard child. I am convinced the child is a bastard long before he is even conceived if he is reared in the KOD.

My great-grandfather had no love for my grandfather. My grandfather hated my father *(it is rumored, although never really confirmed, that he tried to kill him as a youth by allegedly throwing him down a well in Alabama)*. My father, in turn, had no relationship or love for me. He was hateful and violent. My father's heart was never turned toward me. His life has been tough. In truth, my heart has never been turned toward him either.

The crisis in spirituality for the father's is that they have abandoned their first love: the fear of the Lord (Proverbs 9:10): *"The fear of the Lord is the beginning of* ***wisdom****, And the knowledge of the Holy One is* ***understanding.****"*

NO FEAR = NO WISDOM, KNOWLEDGE OR UNDERSTANDING

I have been married for 37 years to the love of my life. Olivia is an amazing woman who loves the Lord and fears Him as well. Having suffered the pains of a fractured household, growing up in a single parent household without a father, it was imperative that I create a stable and loving environment for my children. My son, Nicholas II and my daughter, Taylor have my heart and I know that I have theirs! My granddaughter Kennedy has my heart and I know that I have hers. She is delightful! My family is my sanctuary.

In the gospel of Luke 1:17, the archangel Gabriel prophesied the birth of John the Baptist declaring that he would be the predecessor of Jesus and that he would, *"...Go before Him in the spirit and power of Elijah to turn the hearts of the fathers to* ***the children*** *and the disobedient to the wisdom of the just, to make ready a people prepared for the Lord."*

This prophecy has a different spin on it than the one given in the Book of Malachi. In Malachi, the focus appears to be on the ***family*** and the intimate exchange that would happen between a father and his own children. But in Luke, the emphasis here appears to be more ***tribal or communal*** in that the spirit would provoke ***all of the fathers to turn their hearts toward all of the children*** and embrace the spirit of community as they built the grace KOG in the earth.

The Spirit of the Groom

"I will greatly rejoice in the Lord, My soul shall be joyful in my God; For He has clothed me with the garments of salvation, He has covered me with the robe of righteousness, As a bridegroom decks himself with ornaments, And as a bride adorns herself with her jewels."

(Isaiah 61:10)

I took God's warning seriously about the actions of Elijah in the Book of Malachi. I was committed to my marriage, but I had to learn how to become both a husband and a father. I learned how to be a ***bride*** from studying Christ! I could therefore teach my ***bride*** how to become a ***wife*** by graduating from a ***groom*** to a ***husband*** (John 3:29).

The groom ***loves the wedding*** but is not committed to the ***marriage***. He is an adulterer, a philanderer and a deceiver. He vacillates between good and evil. The bride ***really loves the wedding*** but is not committed to the marriage. She is contentious and restlesses, spoiled and lazy. No wonder so many carnal marriages end in divorce.

Christian marriages do not fare any better than secular marriages. About thirty eight percent (38%) of Christian marriages end in divorce and the divorce rate for subsequent marriages is nearly double the divorce rate for first marriages. Why is this debacle happening within the BOC? It is because of the spirit of the groom. The groom is not married to Christ. As I stated earlier in this chapter, the groom is an adulterer and a philanderer. He is not faithful to the Lord God and engages in every manner of frivolity known to man. He is cold and he is calculating and he is ruthless in his pursuit of the desires of the flesh.

The groom must consume Christ and must be consumed by Him. The groom must be focused on the marriage and not the wedding. As a bride of Christ, the bridegroom must learn the gift of ***submission*** (which, in actuality, is ***service*** not ***slavery***). The WOG teaches married people about the spirit of submission and love in (Ephesians 5:15-33):

"See then that you ***walk circumspectly****, not as fools but as wise, redeeming the time, because the days are evil.*

Therefore do not be unwise, but understand what the will of the Lord is. And ***do not be drunk with wine****, in which is dissipation; but* ***be filled with the Spirit****, speaking to one another in psalms and hymns and spiritual songs, singing and making melody in your heart to the Lord,* ***giving thanks always for all things to God*** *the Father in the name of our Lord Jesus Christ,* <u>***submitting to one another in the fear of God.***</u>

Marriage—Christ and the Church

"Wives, ***submit to your own husbands****, as to the Lord. For the husband is head of the wife, as also Christ is head of the church; and He is the Savior of the body. Therefore, just as the church is subject to Christ, so let the wives be to their own husbands in everything. Husbands,* ***love your wives****, just as Christ also loved the church and gave Himself for her, that He might sanctify and cleanse her with the washing of water by the word, that He might present her to Himself a glorious church, not having spot or wrinkle or any such thing, but that she should be holy and without blemish. So husbands ought to love their own wives as their own bodies;* ***he who loves his wife loves himself****. For no one ever hated his own flesh, but nourishes and cherishes it, just as the Lord does the church.* ***For we are members of His body, of His flesh and of His bones.*** *"For*

this reason a man shall leave his father and mother and be joined to his wife, and ***the two shall become one flesh.****" This is a great mystery, but I speak concerning Christ and the church. Nevertheless let each one of you in particular so love his own wife as himself, and let the wife see that she respects her husband."*

Don't be fooled; marriage is hard work! It requires a lot of time, effort, humility and sacrifice. In this spirit, ***sacrifice*** means ***"the very best you have to give at all times."*** Give your spouse your best offering of submission (service) and grace (spiritual gifts). Your reward will be immeasurable and your life will be filled with peace, love and joy in the HS.

Chapter Seven:
The Spirit of the Unseen Thing

"Now faith is the substance of things hoped for, the evidence of things not seen. For by it the elders obtained a good testimony.
By faith we understand that the worlds were framed by the word of God, so that ***the things which are seen were not made of things which are visible."***

(Hebrews 11:1-3)

Faith is believing in the Unseen Thing (UT); the evidence of or proof of a thing. The worlds were framed by the Word of God (WOG) or faith. The dunamis (dynamic, explosive) power of revelation or, specifically, what releases it is belief in the UT. Since 96% of what exists is unseen and only 4% of what exists is seen, it is imperative that a man has faith. Hebrews 11:6 states, *"Without* ***faith*** *(belief in the UT) it is impossible to please God."*

The UT is everything outside of the realm of what is both known and proven by mankind. It supersedes all human theories, postulates and predictions. Everything inside and outside of the creation of the earth is deemed proprietary knowledge (PK). We made a cursory examination of PK earlier in this book, but I wanted to go a little deeper in this chapter and illustrate its connection to the UT.

As we mentioned before, PK is reserved for the heart and mind of God. I simply love the Amplified version of Hebrews 11:1-3:

"Now faith is the assurance (title deed, confirmation) of things hoped for (divinely guaranteed), and the evidence of things not seen [the conviction of their reality— ***faith comprehends as fact what cannot be experienced by the physical senses]****. For by this [kind of] faith the men of old gained [divine] approval. By faith [that is, with an inherent*

trust and enduring confidence in the power, wisdom and goodness of God] we understand that the worlds (universe, ages) were framed and created [formed, put in order, and equipped for their intended purpose] by the word of God, so that what is seen was not made out of things which are visible."

You have to be dead to miss that! What we see is not really what is (or what it appears to be). It is what God wants us to ***hear, not see*** (Romans 10:17). For example, you may get a bad report from the doctor who tells you that you have a sickness but God told you that you are healed (Isaiah 53:5). What do you choose to believe? By the UT, you have received the promise of divine healing (Malachi 4:2). You can't escape the paradigm of faith in the KOG because faith comprehends as fact what cannot be experienced by the physical senses. The only thing you need to do is believe in God's Word to live a victorious life in the grace of KOG.

Eternity begins at the very end of human knowledge and wisdom and goes on ***in perpetuity.*** PK, as the primary focus in Genesis 1, gives us a snapshot of the beginning of our universe, not of the expanse of the bigness of God. Our galaxy is 20 billion years old and our solar system is a mere 4 billion years in existence. You have to ask yourself, "What preceded 20 billion years ago?"

Take all the great minds of the ages and compare 6,000 years of human history to whatever preceded 20 billion years ago and ask yourself how can I not believe in the UT? I love the fact that God knew exactly what distance to place the sun from the earth to create a sustainable environment for all life forms to flourish. Did you know that it only takes eight minutes for a ray of light to travel 93 million miles from the sun to planet earth? That's 186,000 miles per second! Just think about that for a minute. God created something that can travel 186,000 miles in the blink of an eye! Amen goes there...

In Acts 1:7, we read, "*And He said to them, "It is not for you to know times or seasons which the Father has put in His own authority.*" This statement clearly outlines the intent of PK. ***The HS represents the permanence of God in the life of a Believer.*** There is no underestimating the sovereignty of God through the administration of the HS. The crowning moment in our spiritual odyssey is receiving the deposit of the HS. When, where, how and why it happens is all under the authority of the HS through the application of PK and the UT.

The mandate of faith is not just being ***comfortable*** with not knowing (what God knows) but, rather, being ***passionate*** about not knowing. We do not exist to prove God answers prayers or to live a teflon life, we are here on the earth to be living monuments of God's Grace (John 16:33).

The Spirit of the New Life

"Jesus answered and said to him, "Most assuredly, I say to you, unless one is born again, he cannot see the kingdom of God."

(John 3:3)

"To be born again is always an option when a man is old enough to die." What a revelation given to me by the HS in August 2009. The Believer receives unto himself the new life that was never within his grasp before. The new life manifests itself in conscious repentance and holiness (John 1:12). The old man reconciles himself to death when he has come to the end of himself in thought and deed. He has exhausted every human resource only to wade in a quagmire of futility and anguish. There is something very important you should know about a man that has been redeemed (put on a new life); he has to be given something to do (he must put his hands to the plow).

The question arises, *"Is my knowledge of Jesus born of internal spiritual discernment or only from what I have heard listening to others?"* It is essential that I have a spiritual connection to Christ as my Lord and Savior. To be ***"born again"*** means that ***I hear Christ!***

Do I seek signs of the KOG or do I perceive ***God's rulership?*** It is critical that I am able to discern ***God's nature*** (Philippians 4:7, Colossians 3:16, Ephesians 3:16-19). God's nature and God's rulership have a symbiotic relationship (1 John 3:9). One of the spiritual crises for the new life is ***unforgiveness.***

A close friend of mine once told me a profound truth that I will never forget. He said, ***"You know that your love is intact when you can't be offended."*** The typical response to offense is anger, dismay and unforgiveness. We are in a war; a spiritual war. The natural man causes the spiritual man to sink. Adversity and conflict elicit turmoil in the life of a person. It forces them into dark places, doing dark things with dark people. The spiritual man will then ask the natural man, *"When will you go back to the grave and dig up the **familiar*** (the **sin** that made you **comfortable** when you were living in darkness before you put on your new life)?"

The Spiritual Crisis of Kings and Priests

*"...To Him who loved us and washed us from our sins in His own blood, and has made us **kings and priests** to His God and Father, to Him be glory and dominion forever and ever. Amen."*

(Revelation 1:5-6)

I remember when I first heard someone preach on the topic of kings and priests, I was very young in Christ. I just couldn't make the connection to my personal life and my fledgling spiritual walk. Over time, as I delved into the WOG, I became more skilled in the revelation knowledge of the depth of the two offices and realized that some in the body are ***kings***, some are ***priests*** and strangely enough, some are ***both.***

Why is this a crisis you might ask? Because, sadly, too many Christians never discover or walk in the gift of either office having been diverted to other ministries within the BOC or just simply attending church with no purpose. These are two critical roles in the advancement of the KOG. ***Priests are the visionaries.*** They are led by the HS to see the things of God, to outline a spirit led plan and to select the people necessary to execute the plan successfully.

Kings are the provisionaries. These are the men and women with various skill sets, gifts and talents that will help to finance the KOG. They are the bankers, real estate developers, lawyers, doctors and business people with the acute financial acumen needed to undergird God's vision for His people to infiltrate and destroy the KID!

For example, the Outreach Ministry needs a small apartment building to house single mothers who are victims of domestic violence. The priests put together a plan to relocate, train and protect the mothers and their children including food, clothing, shelter and security. The kings, in turn, will identify, purchase, renovate, furnish, stock and secure the premises for the families. The priests (non-exclusive to pastors) can also be elders, laity and deacons. They are the people with the gift of hospitality, prayer, peace, wisdom and patience. The kings will train the mothers on finding jobs, budgeting, parenting and mentoring to help them get back on their feet.

Divine teamwork and mutual respect between both entities is paramount in order to achieve maximum success in ministry. It is crucial that the BOC not try to make priests out of every man and kings must be cultivated through education, training, practical application and commerce. It is essential that business and entrepreneurship finance

God's vision for a glorious kingdom. Pushing all men into the priesthood would severely upset the balance of vision and provision.

Unfulfilled kings become ***"spectators"*** and, eventually, ***"dropouts"*** because their spirit man is in crisis as a result of their inability to walk out their gifts. There is an intense need for the priests to genuinely honor, bless and develop a partnership with kings so that they feel free to go to war for the KOG.

God made men to thrive on conquest and engagement. When men view their lives as vital and relevant, there is a cataclysmic response inside of their spirit man. Something changes as they morph into a spirit of peace. For the king, their battlefield is the marketplace and they have the fortitude of warriors to provide for the BOC and boldly advance the KOG.

Do not be deluded by ***obscurity***; your heart, mind, body and spirit must be crisis free and pure toward what God is saying:

"Take My yoke upon you and learn from Me [following Me as My disciple], for I am gentle and humble in heart, and you will find rest (renewal, blessed quiet) for your souls. For My yoke is easy [to bear] and My burden is light." (Matthew 11:29-30 AMP)

Spiritual Famine for the Word of God

*"Behold, the days are coming," says the Lord God, "That I will send a **famine** on the land, not a famine of bread, nor a thirst for water, But of **hearing the words of the Lord.** They shall wander from sea to sea, And from north to east; They shall run to and fro, seeking the word of the Lord, But shall not find it."*

(Amos 8:11-12)

We don't hear much about this cat called Amos in church. He is referred to as one of the "minor" prophets in the WOG. But if you have ever read the Book of Amos, you will know that there is ***nothing*** minor about this brother! He was a Judean sheep breeder with a strong message for Israel amidst the backdrop of extreme paganism and idol worship.

He prophesied a famine of God's Word which was a searing indictment on the wayward character of God's people. Amos' tenure as an oracle for God was short lived (from 755-754 B.C.) as he ventured to Bethel from his hometown of Tekoa, delivered the prophetic oracles (dropped it like it was hot) and returned home to tend his sheep and harvest his sycamore fig trees. Amos was not a wealthy man, but he was passionately devoted to service in the Judean wilderness.

The spiritual famine for God's Word (WOG) is centered around the spirit of ***injustice*** reigning in the earth. Justice is relational and is a hallmark of the WOG. It promotes good relations between groups and individuals and it quells anger, hostility and violence. Injustice breeds alienation and contempt and fosters ill will among the brethren. Injustice builds walls and shackles the spirit of love.

The WOG and the Voice of God (VOG) have a spirit of similitude (parallelism). They function under the banner of: ***seed*** (word planted), ***time*** (word cultivated) and ***harvest*** (word manifested). God releases His Word from eternity into time to an oracle. The person receives the Word and moves quickly to execute what God has told Him to say or do. After a certain period of time, the thing which God said will come to pass and the harvest or desired result will be apparent.

How do you know you are hearing the voice of God? The VOG is an inner spirit that regulates our behavior and decision making and tells us if we are on a righteous path or in need of correction. Developing our spiritual sense to hear the VOG occurs through practical application (prayer, meditation and supplication) and ***active listening*** (keeping your mouth shut)! You will gain the ability to discern good and evil voices. You will learn to shut down your personal opinion, turn down the world's volume (distractions) and mute evil desires and provocations:

"For though by this time you ought to be teachers, you need someone to teach you again the first principles of the oracles of God; and you have come to need milk and not solid food. For everyone who partakes only of milk is unskilled in the word of righteousness, for he is a babe. But solid food belongs to those who are of full age, that is, those who by reason of use have their senses exercised to discern both good and evil." (Hebrews 5:12-14)

In the KOG, private success translates into public triumph. In other words, an intimate, consistent and fervent spiritual exchange with the HS will train you for battle in the marketplace. Your one-on-one tutorials with the Spirit of Truth will prepare you for righteousness and holiness. You will be transformed from ***goats*** (rebellion) into ***sheep*** (humility). But the greatest benefit of discernment of the Spirit is the gift of entering into His ***rest*** (peace):

"Therefore, as the Holy Spirit says: "Today, if you will hear His voice, do not harden your hearts as in the rebellion, in the day of trial in the wilderness, Where your fathers tested Me, tried Me, and saw My works forty years. Therefore I was angry with that generation, And said, 'They always go astray in their heart, and they have not known My ways.' So I swore in My wrath, 'They shall not enter My rest.' " (Hebrews 3:7-12)

There are several things that will ***<u>mute the VOG</u>*** in your life. They are habitual sin and iniquity (premeditated sin); Isaiah 59:2; Psalm 68:18; lack of repentance; generational sin; rebellion and stubbornness (1 Samuel 15:23); unbelief and offense (Mark 6:1-6); preoccupation with things of the world (2 Timothy 2:4). A wise man once said, ***"That which you can't give away has mastered you!"***

Conversely, there are also several things that you can do to increase your ***<u>ability to hear the VOG</u>***. They include:

1. Making a decision to draw closer to God by developing a deeper spiritual relationship (James 4:8);
2. Repent of your sins and transgressions (Acts 2:38);
3. Make your mind "still" (quiet your thoughts until they become His thoughts) (Habakkuk 2:1);
4. Pray in the Spirit (close your eyes, shut your mouth, open your ears and heart and listen for the VOG); (Ephesians 1:18), (1 Corinthians 4:14);
5. Renew your mind (Ephesians 4:23), (Colossians 3:16), (Romans 12:1-2), (James 1:22);
6. Be attentive to the still small VOG not allowing the cares of this world to distract you or disrupt your fellowship;
7. Be mindful of how God speaks to you: through dreams, visions, spontaneous impressions, conversations with others, the HS or the WOG.

The VOG is a peace that settles your spirit man; it bears witness in your spirit with His own Spirit. It is spiritual confirmation when the sound you hear agrees with His written word and it never contradicts what the HS has told you.

If you are experiencing a famine for the WOG, it is your own fault. The WOG is free and more accessible than anytime before in human history. What ends a famine? Seed, time and harvest! Amen.

The Pitfalls of a Spiritual Maze

"There is therefore now no condemnation to those who are in Christ Jesus, who do not walk according to the flesh, but

according to the Spirit. For the law of the Spirit of life in Christ Jesus has made me free from the law of sin and death. For what the law could not do in that it was weak through the flesh, God did by sending His own Son in the likeness of sinful flesh, on account of sin: He condemned sin in the flesh..."

(Romans 8:1-3)

A maze is defined as *a network of paths and hedges designed as a puzzle through which one has to find a way.* It also means *to be* ***dazed or confused.***

A man that pursues the lust of the flesh is subject to (controlled and manipulated by) sin to the point of the inability to recognize what they are doing. With every turn in a maze you will encounter a wall. Inside of a maze, there are no directions for you to follow. In a maze, a ***mouse*** (type and shadow of a man) never stops or reflects, he just hits one wall after the other. A scientist sits patiently and monitors its behavior.

God's vantage point in our lives is the same as the scientist who is observing the mouse. God can easily see the way of escape (1 Corinthians 10:1-13). God has afforded each of us a way of escape from temptation through the power of the HS. He has also given us examples of what has happened to those who have fallen prey to temptation.

The only way out of this spiritual crisis is for the hand of God to reach down and lift us out of the maze through the leading of the Holy Spirit.

Every turn in a maze is met with another wall. In a maze, a ***lab rat*** (a man who is reliant on his own strength) never stops moving; he never stops and reflects, he just hits one brick wall after another.

The purpose of a maze is to create suffering and torture. In ancient Egyptian times, mazes were used to bewilder their prisoners. They frustrated, confused and infuriated their captives. A maze is a complex series of passages. These passages themselves fork and eventually do one of only two things: either they come to a "dead end" (Satan) or the passage closes in on the lab rat in a loop with itself or connects with another passage separate from itself that does not provide a solution (escape). There is usually "only one correct path" (the Lord God) in the maze from start to finish.

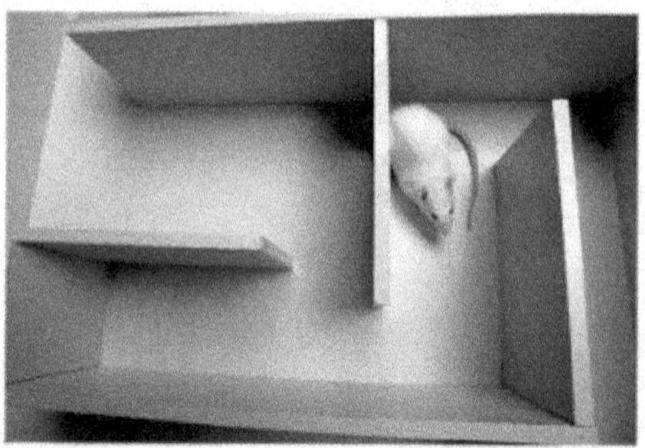

There are countless Christians who have succumbed to the lure of the enemy. They become crushed by the lusts of the flesh, the lusts of the eyes and the pride of life. Jesus as the way of escape recreates the sinner into a Believer, a friend and a son. He is transformed into the physical and spiritual embodiment of the ***"condemnation of sin"*** by his words, walk and witness. As a result, he now has the very same ability as Christ; that is, to ***condemn sin in the flesh!*** Amen to the glory of God!

Chapter Eight:
The Spirit of the Fruit and the Flesh

*"It is the Spirit who gives life; the **flesh** profits nothing. The words that I speak to you are spirit, and they are life. But there are some of you who do not believe." For Jesus knew from the beginning who they were who did not believe, and who would betray Him."*

(John 6:63-64)

The Believer has to develop a certain attitude toward the things of the flesh. Many times over my life as a Believer, the HS has awakened me from my sleep to drop a nugget in my spirit. In January 2001 He said to me, ***"When I gave you My faith, it was perfect. As soon as My faith touched your flesh, it (My faith) became perforated."*** Over the past few years, each victory in my walk fills a hole (repairs the breech). However, each act of fear, doubt and/or rebellion creates another hole. Without faith, it is impossible to please God (Hebrews 11:6).

In the Greek language, ***faith*** is translated ***"pistis"*** #4102, Strong's Concordance. It means persuasion, credence (moral conviction) of religious (spiritual) truth, or the truthfulness of God; reliance upon Christ for ***"soteria"*** (salvation); constancy, assurance, believe, fidelity, sure, true; also, ***"peitho"*** #3982, to rely on (by inward certainty), to have confidence, to wax (be made confident); obey and yield.

The Book of Galatians was an indictment on the blatant bastardization of the gospel of Jesus Christ among the Judaizers. Paul refuted every move with a more compelling, passionate and truthful revelation of the gift of salvation through faith in God as the only way to achieve eternal life. He asserted that "works" alone were futile and arose from the flesh. Galatians 5:16-26 says:

"I say then: Walk in the Spirit, and you shall not fulfill the lust of the flesh. For the flesh lusts against the Spirit, and the Spirit against the flesh; and these are contrary to one another, so that you do not do the things that you wish. But if you are led by the Spirit, you are not under the law.

Now ***the works of the flesh*** *are evident, which are: adultery, fornication, uncleanness, lewdness, idolatry, sorcery, hatred, contentions, jealousies, outbursts of wrath, selfish ambitions, dissensions, heresies, envy, murders, drunkenness, revelries, and the like; of which I tell you beforehand, just as I also told you in time past, that those who practice such things will not inherit the kingdom of God.*

But ***the fruit of the Spirit*** *is love, joy, peace, longsuffering, kindness, goodness, faithfulness, gentleness, self-control. Against such there is no law. And those who are Christ's have crucified the flesh with its passions and desires. If we live in the Spirit, let us also walk in the Spirit. Let us not become conceited, provoking one another, envying one another."*

The Book of Genesis identifies Ishmael as a "son of the flesh" and Isaac as a "son of the Spirit"from the very beginning. This was where the war of the flesh and the spirit began. The Holy Spirit is the promise of God (the Comforter) and He added that our human bodies would be the container or host of the HS. *The "**flesh**" is a **pattern of living** (our habits) and **<u>is not your physical body.</u>***

The Book of (2 Peter 2:19-22) aptly states this truth: ***You cannot will yourself to a victory over the flesh:***

"While they promise them liberty, they themselves are slaves of corruption; for by whom a person is overcome, by him also he is brought into bondage. For if, after they have escaped the pollutions of the world through the knowledge of the Lord and Savior Jesus Christ, they are again entangled in them and overcome, the latter end is worse for them than the beginning. For it would have been better for them not to have known the way of righteousness, than having known it, to turn from the holy commandment delivered to them. But it has happened to them according to the true proverb: "A dog returns to his own vomit," and, "a sow, having washed, to her wallowing in the mire."

The HS told me a profound truth many years ago. With regard to our dalliances in and out of the Spirit, ***"The flesh never forgets!"*** The apostle Paul outlines the treacherous ambiguity that rages inside each of us on a daily basis as we fight off the attacks of the enemy in both the spirit and natural realms. The flesh can ***only*** be overcome by the Spirit (Romans 7:15-20 AMP version):

"For I do not understand my own actions [I am baffled and bewildered by them]. I do not practice what I want to do, but I am doing the very thing I hate [and yielding to my human nature, my worldliness—my sinful capacity]. Now if I habitually do what I do not want to do, [that means] I agree with the Law, confessing that it is good (morally excellent). So now [if that is the case, then] it is no longer I who do it [the disobedient thing which I despise], but the sin [nature] which lives in me. For I know that nothing good lives in me, that is, in my flesh [my human nature, my worldliness—my sinful capacity]. For the willingness [to do good] is present in me, but the doing of good is not. For the good that I want to do, I do not

do, but I practice the very evil that I do not want. But if I am doing the very thing I do not want to do, I am no longer the one doing it [that is, it is not me that acts], but the sin [nature] which lives in me."

The Anatomy of Sin

The revelation that the flesh is our habits not our bodies may be shocking to some people. However, there are three types of sin: ***sensual sin, superstitious sin and social sin:***

1. Sensual sin: (sin inflicted upon ourselves): adultery, fornication, lewdness, revelries (orgies), uncleanness, drunkenness;
2. Superstitious sin: (sin against God): idolatry (anyone or anything worshipped before God); Bible Deists are bible worshippers who love the Book but don't know the God who authored the Book; drugs, witchcraft, sorcery;
3. Social sin: (sin against other people): hatred (attitude of the mind that defies and challenges others), dissensions, contentions, wrath, heresies, envy, jealousies and murders.

In this scripture, Paul is teaching us about our ***habits*** as Unbelievers, not as an isolated incident but as a premeditated choice conducted routinely. God wants us to do good versus not just doing evil (the Pharisees avoided evil, but they didn't do anything good either). (Matthew 5:17-20) and (Luke 6:27-42) support the fact that God desires for us to actively pursue good in our daily lives.

The love of God produces joy in the life of the Believer which leads to peace (rest). You cannot lose joy if it is real; if, for some reason you lose joy, it was probably happiness because happiness is temporary. However, the joy of the Lord is eternal. This is the fruit from God.

The fruit toward mankind is ***long suffering,*** which is the courageous endurance of others without giving up on them and not complaining about it. It is gentleness and kindness (placing others before yourself) and goodness which is love in action.

The fruit that develops toward us is centered around faithfulness (dependability), meekness (power under control); and self control (patience, peace and perspective). The apostle Paul called the confluence of these elements ***"Resurrection Power."*** This is the power given to us to seek the lost; this power is hidden from the natural eye. Fellowship is the perfect climate for the fruit of the spirit to flourish and cannot prosper without the seed of faith.

Sin is the adversary of the seed of faith seeking to choke it out at the ***root*** (the peak of ***brokenness*** [lowest point] in the life of the Believer). The remedy for sin is incessant fellowship with the Father. Speaking to Him, praying to Him, serving His people in the marketplace, writing to Him and listening to Him will diffuse the power of the devil. The WOG will surgically remove sin from your anatomy (heart, mind, body and soul) and place you firmly on a path toward healing and incomparable spiritual growth and maturity.

The Spirit of Carnality

"Therefore put to death your members which are on the earth: fornication, uncleanness, passion, evil desire, and covetousness, which is idolatry. Because of these things the wrath of God is coming upon the sons of disobedience, in which you yourselves once walked when you lived in them. But now you yourselves are to put off all these: anger, wrath, malice, blasphemy, filthy language out of your mouth. Do not lie to one another, since you have put off the old man with his deeds, and have put on the new man who is renewed in knowledge according to the image of Him who created him, where there is

neither Greek nor Jew, circumcised nor uncircumcised, barbarian, Scythian, slave nor free, but Christ is all and in all."

(Colossians 3:5-11)

The word carnal or carnality means fleshly lust or an inherited nature that wars against God. The carnal spirit wants to live without God's moral and spiritual compass. It does not want to be told what to do and it is narcissistic. The way a person understands this subject has much to do with their theology (belief or non-belief in God, salvation, faith, love, hope, life and death).

The Greek words for carnality are ***"sarx"*** (flesh as opposed to the spirit; it also can denote an attitude or physical part of the body) and ***"sarkikos"*** (carnal or fleshly). **Our physical flesh is not sinful**. It is our carnal mind that corrupts the flesh. The flesh will only do what the mind tells it to do. The flesh does not act independently of the mind. The flesh is taught to like (desire) certain sinful activity by both exposure and experimentation. This is called ***whetting the appetite.*** In other words, this is ***learned behavior***.

The carnal part of our fleshly existence is called ***inbred sin*** or ***original depravity*** (the transgression that created a void between Adam and God in the Garden) that is a corrupt state of the heart that opposes God and the spirit of holiness. In the unregenerate person, this state of heart is not only contrary to the will of God, but must always continue as such, unless God moves upon it with His Gracious Spirit to diffuse it or alter its course.

Inbred sin is what the Apostle speaks about in the Book of Hebrews, 12th chapter: ***"The sin that doth so easily beset you."*** It (the sin) fits us as well as a custom made suit; these are the seeds of sin because all outward or actual transgressions spring forth from it. This is a law of our being; a law simply being a power or method of working. He states in Romans 7:21: ***"I find then a law, that, when I would do good, evil is present with me."***

This response to the lure of sin represents the universal consciousness and testimony of our humanity- an original disposition, deep-seated in the bowels of the soul, that contends continually with our moral spirit sense. In each of our souls the voice of Satan reverberates against the walls of righteousness, holiness and peace appealing to our carnal desires working in concert with the lusts of the eyes, the lusts of the flesh and the pride of life.

The sound of his voice is like a thunderous stampede of horses surging across an open plain to avoid captivity. But it is that same voice that is seeking the weaker vessel to captivate, seduce and manipulate his spirit man. Satan's claim to our mortal bodies is in harmony with our corrupted hearts making it easy to corral the wayward soul.

This is what makes men such defenseless targets and is the source of much of their sorrows and calamities. It is the root of much of the opposition of this world to godliness. It (the carnal mind) is the spirit that led men to crucify the Son of God and it will be the chief element of hell, and is the hell that has already begun in the soul of many, while in this carnal life, restrained and thwarted many times only by environments, circumstances or Divine Intervention. Selah...

Chapter Nine
The Spirit of Relevance

"Then Lot went up out of Zoar and dwelt in the mountains, and his two daughters were with him; for he was afraid to dwell in Zoar. And he and his two daughters dwelt in a cave. Now the firstborn said to the younger, "Our father is old, and there is no man on the earth to come in to us as is the custom of all the earth. Come, let us make our father drink wine, and we will lie with him, that we may preserve the lineage of our father." So they made their father drink wine that night. And the firstborn went in and lay with her father, and he did not know when she lay down or when she arose.

It happened on the next day that the firstborn said to the younger, "Indeed I lay with my father last night; let us make him drink wine tonight also, and you go in and lie with him, that we may preserve the lineage of our father." Then they made their father drink wine that night also. And the younger arose and lay with him, and he did not know when she lay down or when she arose.

Thus both the daughters of Lot were with child by their father. The firstborn bore a son and called his name Moab; he is the father of the Moabites to this day. And the younger, she also bore a son and called his name Ben-Ammi; he is the father of the people of Ammon to this day."

(Genesis 19:30-38)

The spirit of Moab is a type of the BOC. It is incestuous, wicked, manipulative and self-serving. In the Hebrew language, the name ***Moab*** means ***"he is of my father,"*** a sordid reminder of its genesis. Lot's two daughters conspired to have sex with their father because they were isolated from civilization living in a cave outside of Zoar out of fear. His daughters were lonely and needed the intimacy of men. There were no men in their midst. So they plied Lot with wine, had sex with him and both became pregnant with sons; the older daughter named her son

Moab (Moabites) and the younger daughter named her son Ben-Ammi (Ammonites).

All the definitive attributes, characteristics and glaring depravity connected to the spirit of Moab are rooted and grounded in our inherent need as humans to be ***relevant.*** Relevance is an incessant pursuit of the general populous and has precipitated a hard pivot away from the spirit of humility, modesty and decency. People violate every aspect of human decorum consistently in order to be relevant. Of course, hypocrisy, arrogance and impropriety are the undertow of relevance in our modern society.

The spirit of Moab has infiltrated the modern day church and contaminated many of its leaders and laity. The preachers, priests and potentates have all been tried in the court of public opinion and convicted as guilty for sins against the BOC under the guise of relevance. They have systematically bastardized the gospel of the KOG for ***mammon.*** They have propped themselves up as the oracles of Christ Jesus with smoke and mirrors, sleight of hand and other cheap magic tricks in real time. They have saddled the backs of their broken congregations and drained their feeble bank accounts for all their worth while creating insulated fiefdoms for them and their lackeys.

His daughters were desperate and carnal in their resolution to satisfy their flesh. Their perverted ambition perpetuated two convoluted bloodlines. They compromised the integrity of the institution of the family and tainted their father's legacy until this very day. After two thousand years, we are still talking about their vile act of treason against their father.

Why trick your father and manipulate him into an unconscionable act unless you are filled with bile yourself? Lot's daughters are a mirror of the BOC. They were restless, selfish and unruly. They had hidden agendas and no respect for authority. They were led by their father the devil into unthinkable deviousness and immorality. Lot was burdened with the shame of raising children born out of incest and his wife was the "poster child" of ***disobedience*** and paid for it with her life. The spirit of disobedience is transferable and his daughters wallowed in it.

The spirit of relevance is comparable to a ***kingdom***; it must have a strategy for its ***development, defense and destiny.*** The individual engages the various channels he might take toward the goal of relevance (unilateral acceptance). He begins by identifying what is ***"trending"***on social media, does a little research, develops a platform and then jumps in with both feet. Once immersed in the daily rigors of tweets, postings and instagram pics and videos, he is well on his way to creating ***followers*** (kingdom subjects) who support and ***defend*** his position.

Once an individual has amassed a large following, they are empowered to engage the adversary (whoever or whatever it might be) in full attack mode. Their ***"cause"*** may or may not be legitimate; that doesn't matter as much as how much they sway the critical masses to agree with their position. Relevance in today's society is more about believability than righteousness. It's more about band aids than true healing; sound bites and rhetoric than truth and life, and self promotion than humility. The individual or group must defend their position at all costs. They have fully committed to the platform and there's no turning back!

Inherent in many of these ***"movements"*** are pockets of individuals that have to be the voice of reason. These are the people that have witnessed the "message" veer dangerously off course and are compelled to challenge all existing paradigms that have the temerity to deviate from its original intent and design. Who is the leader of the movement? Is it Felix Rodriguez or is it Christ? Is it Mary Jenkins or is it the Holy Spirit?

Once we get past the prayer vigil and the moment of silence, how much do we involve the Spirit of Truth in our decisions, direction and purpose? After the murals are painted, tee shirts printed and flowers left at the makeshift altar on the street corner, what is the next move? How does the looting, senseless murders and random acts of violence contribute to the goal of relevance?

This is the part of the ***defense strategy*** that puzzles me. This sounds a lot like Lot's daughters getting their father drunk so they could have sex with him in order to perpetuate their fanily's bloodline. Nevermind the flashing lights and clashing cymbals of "incest" echoing throughout history or the evil and wicked mindsets that conjured up the notion in the first place. Integrity be damned; we are gonna have these babies no matter what! It was Lot's daughter's obsession with how their ***destiny*** would be recorded that contaminated the waters of righteousness and dignity.

The inherent problem with destiny is that man cannot control it. He has bastardized and manipulated the events of earthly life to try and create the future he wants or frame the picture he paints to fit in a nice, tidy box with a bow. Then LIFE happens; let's call it ***"true"destiny*** (the ***unseen thing*** that God controls through the power of the HS). He doesn't understand that ***yesterday, today and tomorrow are all the same*** (this observation falls under the aegis of ***quantum mechanics and proprietary knowledge*** that we covered earlier in this book) in the eyes of God.

In the spiritual continuum, our entire lives have been played out before we enter into the earth realm. In other words, we were with God in the beginning as spirit material. We were then dispatched into the earth with an assignment through our mother's womb. We experience natural life (wickedness) and then spiritual life (redemption) and walk out God's plan that He purposed in us from the foundation of the world (Matthew 25:34). We bear the mark of Christ as sons and we transcend this natural life having fulfilled our

true destiny to be ***witnesses*** of the Gospel of Peace to the world (Acts 1:8) and rejoin the Father in eternity.

Spiritual destiny is a continuous sequence of events scripted by God in which adjacent elements are not perceptibly different from each other in real time through limited human wisdom and sight. But to the HS, the ***extremes*** (man's wisdom and knowledge versus God's wisdom and knowledge) are quite distinct and are the proof of His infinite presence, power and love. Amen.

"For I know the thoughts that I think toward you, says the Lord, thoughts of peace and not of evil, to give you a future and a hope."

(Jeremiah 29:11)

The Spirit of the Furnace

"Therefore at that time certain Chaldeans came forward and accused the Jews. They spoke and said to King Nebuchadnezzar, "O king, live forever! You, O king, have made a decree that everyone who hears the sound of the horn, flute, harp, lyre, and psaltery, in symphony with all kinds of music, shall fall down and worship the gold image; and whoever does not fall down and worship shall be cast into the midst of a burning fiery furnace. There are certain Jews whom you have set over the affairs of the province of Babylon: Shadrach, Meshach, and Abed-Nego; these men, O king, have not paid due regard to you. They do not serve your gods or worship the gold image which you have set up."

Then Nebuchadnezzar, in rage and fury, gave the command to bring Shadrach, Meshach, and Abed-Nego. So they brought these men before the king. Nebuchadnezzar spoke, saying to them, "Is it true, Shadrach, Meshach, and Abed-Nego, that you do not serve my gods or worship the gold image which I have set up? Now if you are ready at the time you hear the sound of the horn, flute, harp, lyre, and psaltery, in symphony with all kinds of music, and you fall down and worship the image which I have made, good! But if you do not worship, you shall be cast immediately into the midst of a burning fiery furnace. And who is the god who will deliver you from my hands?"

Shadrach, Meshach, and Abed-Nego answered and said to the king, "O Nebuchadnezzar, we have no need to answer you in this matter. If that is the case, our God whom we serve is able to deliver us from the burning fiery furnace, and He will deliver us from your hand, O king. But if not, let it be known to you, O king, that we do not serve your gods, nor will we worship the gold image which you have set up."

Saved in the Fiery Trial

Then Nebuchadnezzar was full of fury, and the expression on his face changed toward Shadrach, Meshach, and Abed-Nego. He spoke and commanded that they heat the furnace seven times more than it was usually heated. And he commanded certain mighty men of valor who were in his army to bind Shadrach, Meshach, and Abed-Nego, and cast them into the burning fiery furnace. Then these men were bound in their coats, their trousers, their turbans, and their other garments, and were cast into the midst of the burning fiery furnace. Therefore, because the king's command was urgent, and the furnace exceedingly hot, the flame of the fire killed those men who took up Shadrach, Meshach, and Abed-Nego. And these three men, Shadrach, Meshach, and Abed-Nego, fell down bound into the midst of the burning fiery furnace.

Then King Nebuchadnezzar was astonished; and he rose in haste and spoke, saying to his counselors, "Did we not cast three men bound into the midst of the fire?" They answered and said to the king, "True, O king."

"Look!" he answered, "I see four men loose, walking in the midst of the fire; and they are not hurt, and the form of the fourth is like the Son of God."

Nebuchadnezzar Praises God

Then Nebuchadnezzar went near the mouth of the burning fiery furnace and spoke, saying, "Shadrach, Meshach, and Abed-Nego, servants of the Most High God, come out, and come here." Then Shadrach, Meshach, and Abed-Nego came from the midst of the fire. And the satraps, administrators, governors, and the king's counselors gathered together, and they saw these men on whose bodies the fire had no power; the hair of their head was not singed nor were their garments affected, and the smell of fire was not on them.

Nebuchadnezzar spoke, saying, "Blessed be the God of Shadrach, Meshach, and Abed-Nego, who sent His Angel and delivered His servants who trusted in Him, and they have frustrated the king's word, and yielded their bodies, that they should not serve nor worship any god except their own God! Therefore I make a decree that any people, nation, or language which speaks anything amiss against the God of Shadrach, Meshach, and Abed-Nego shall be cut in pieces, and their houses shall be made an ash heap; because there is no other God who can deliver like this. Then the king promoted Shadrach, Meshach, and Abed-Nego in the province of Babylon."

(Daniel 3:8-30)

I always say the thing we have most in common with Jesus is the ***gift of adversity***. I call it a gift because surviving adversity and coming through it without the *"smell of smoke on you"* is a badge of honor in the KOG. The ***furnace*** is the proving ground for the sons of God as we offer up ourselves to experience the ***"living death"*** under the direction of the HS. As I stated earlier in this book, the "living death" is the manifestation of the repentance, reconciliation and restoration of the broken soul in real time without physically dying.

It is the Presence of the HS (unlike Jesus who had to physically die) shaping and guiding us through the maze of sin in our lives while equipping us with dunamis power to be able to run the race of service in the marketplace. Make no mistake, it is God Almighty (not the devil) who is allowing the series of calamitous events to occur in your life that will increase or decrease your measure of faith.

The furnace is a spirit. It can be anything, any place or anyone. It is symbolic of an insurmountable impediment in your life that only God can help you to overcome. God is saying to us, *"Don't be afraid of the furnace, I gave man the knowledge to make it. Don't worry about the fire either; I made that too! (See Moses and the burning bush). My Presence is the guarantee of safety and success (Joshua 1:5)."*

What do you look like while you are in the fire? Are you fearful, fretful and pitiful or are you steadfast, immovable and unyielding, always worshipping God? As a Believer you must realize that people are watching you (both Believers and non-Believers) to witness your reaction to the fire and the furnace. The HS has the ability to call you out of the ***fire*** and give you your next assignment. The fire is symbolic of testing, reproving and purging us of the things that so easily beset us. Everyone and everything is made subject to the fire.

How does the fire lose its power? The answer can be found in (Daniel 3:16-18). The man's perspective, belief and knowledge of who God is and what God can or will do to manifest His will in the earth can diffuse the fire. But even if he doesn't do it, His will is still perfect (it does not change because of our circumstances). His will is not going to mutate because I am in distress, but I will change as a result of ***"standing"*** (resisting the temptation to submit to my own will, thoughts and desires). So I exit the furnace in the midst of the fire unscaithed and unflappable. Yet the people look upon me and marvel at what they see (the expectation was for me to be consumed by the fiery furnace) since they have never witnessed anyone survive its stronghold before.

It is man's device to create a snare that he believes is inescapable. Before I broke the shackles of fear in the furnace, it was inescapable. The thing we feared most was so intimidating, we would succumb to it because it had never been conquered before (see David and Goliath). There was nothing I could point to that would give me hope; nothing to quiet my spirit. In that instance, fear triumphed over faith and I was consumed with the former over the latter.

In my mind's eye, the fiery furnace represents systems of this world. Systems that seem insurmountable and paradigms so awesome, the mere pressure or even thought of challenging it is too much to bear. God prepares us to engage these systems through chastisement (humility). We must be ready to do battle at all times as a citizen of the KOG. Successful war deflates the spirit of the adversary. Just think about it for a moment, when you eliminate the ***"alpha male,"*** destroy the citadel and capture the city, the spoils (love, peace and joy in the HS) are yours!

The Spirit of the Fourth Man

*"...Look!" he answered, "I see four men loose, walking in the midst of the fire; and they are not hurt, and **the form of the fourth is like the Son of God.**"*

(Daniel 3:25)

I always wondered what the King saw in the fiery furnace that made him ***know*** that the ***fourth form*** (man) he saw walking around in the fire was like the Son of God. How would he know what the Son of God looked like? In order for the King to come to that conclusion, he obviously had previous knowledge of the existence, power and presence of the Son of God. When he stepped over the dead bodies of the guards who took the three men up to the fire and witnessed them walking around loose in the fire, it had to blow his mind. My Holy Ghost imagination had the three men walking around in prayer and praise that God had spared them for their faith. It is my contention that the King ***heard*** genuine praise out of love and reverence for the King of Glory as opposed to the prefabricated praise he mustered from his kingdom out of fear and intimidation.

The revelation of the Trinity was not fully manifested until Jesus' time on earth, however, the OT records God's preparation of humanity for this truth. These foreshadowings of God or the preincarnate Christ in a visible form are called ***"theophanies"*** or appearances of God. Some examples include (Genesis 16:7-13), (Genesis 18:1-15), (Exodus 3) and (Daniel 7:13).

He also witnessed the ***unity in spirit*** of the three men as they welcomed the Presence of the Son of God in their trouble. The WOG teaches us that faith comes by hearing and that our sense of hearing is sharpened the more we hear, study and meditate on God's Word. So the King ***heard*** and he ***submitte***d to the Presence of God. Pagan cultures did not deny the existence of other gods; but it's one thing to ***hear*** about a monumental event and something entirely different to ***experience*** it for yourself!

There was no spiritual crisis for Shadrach, Meshach and Abed-Nego; they held firm to their faith while looking the most formidable ***faith killer*** (the fiery furnace) dead in the eye without blinking. The spirit of the fourth man represents <u>***restoration***</u>. The three men were given slave names by the chief eunuch over the House of the King and were cast into the fire as ***Shadrach*** ("I am fearful of the god of the King") but came out as ***Hananiah*** ("the Lord is gracious"), ***Meshach*** ("I am of little account") came out as ***Mishael*** ("Who is what God is?") and ***Abed-Nego*** ("servant of the god Nebo") came out as ***Azariah*** ("the Lord has helped me").

The latter are God given names restored to them by faith in the Lord of Hosts. The Fourth Man went before the three men into the fire the moment they released their faith to reject the decree to worship the image of

Nebuchadnezzar. There, He waited for their arrival, defusing the power of the fire and creating an environment of safety in the midst of trouble. Once they entered into the furnace, their bonds were loosed in the Presence of the Son of God, their lives were spared, they astounded the Babylonians and the King was ***humbled by the witness of their faith.***

"No temptation has overtaken you except such as is common to man; but God is faithful, who will not allow you to be tempted beyond what you are able, but with the temptation will also make the way of escape, that you may be able to bear it." (1 Corinthians 10:13)

The main point of this story was never really about the three men, it was about the sovereignty of God; His Presence and His Power. It told the story of how He goes before us, is in trouble with us and delivers us from it through our obedience, faith and sacrifice. God had already made provision for the three men in the fire by the names He had given them from the foundation of the world.

God's name for you (faithful, righteous or holy) will prevail in your most difficult circumstance. The world has many names for you and we all wear them well contingent upon the situation. These names, labels and titles are all snares (they bind us). But when you come face to face with God, whether you believe in Him or not, you will be changed and transformed to comply with the original intent of what God has called you (in my case, Nicholas meaning "victory of the people") and called you to (your destiny).

FAITH + FIRE = REDEMPTION & REFINED

FEAR + FIRE = CONDEMNATION & CONSUMED

The Spirit of Grace and Thorns

"And lest I should be exalted above measure by the abundance of the revelations, a ***thorn in the flesh*** *was given to*

me, a messenger of Satan to buffet me, lest I be exalted above measure. Concerning this thing I pleaded with the Lord three times that it might depart from me. And He said to me, "My ***grace is sufficient for you****, for My strength is made perfect in weakness." Therefore most gladly I will rather boast in my infirmities, that the power of Christ may rest upon me. Therefore I take pleasure in infirmities, in reproaches, in needs, in persecutions, in distresses, for Christ's sake. For when I am weak, then I am strong."*

(2 Corinthians 12:7-10)

When you get right down to the nitty gritty, ***"Grace is a WARNING!"*** The ***thorn*** and ***grace*** are inextricably tied together in the life of a Believer. Both are seeded in the revelation of truth designed to make you free. Simply stated, no thorn, no freedom; no grace, no liberty. The Believer must scream from the highest mountain to whomever will hear him, ***"Tell me the truth if you are to make me free!"***

The ***mantle of rulership in the spirit*** that God has crafted for you is no different than it was for Joshua as he entered into Canaan. God will have the very same conversation with you that he had with Joshua (Joshua 1:1-4), ***"Moses is dead.*** *Don't be deceived, he is not coming back! I am passing the mantle of rulership to you."* In this case, *"Moses"* could be anything or anyone that may have caused you to stumble or anything or anyone that you depended upon more than God.

"...And of His fullness we have all received, and grace for grace." (John 1:16)

"For out of His fullness [the superabundance of His grace and truth] we have all received grace upon grace [spiritual blessing upon spiritual blessing, favor upon favor, and gift heaped upon gift]." (John 1:16/Amplified version).

Remember, I also said that grace is a warning; so to this point, we have also received warning upon warning out of His Fullness. The thorn is the catalyst for change. Like death, it is one of God's ultimate behavior modification tools. Death jars an individual like a train wreck. Like death, the thorn is necessary to keep the Believer focused on the will of God and not the circumstances of everyday life. God doesn't deal with (fix) every aspect of our flawed character at once. Along with His grace comes the requirement of ***spiritual accountability.*** The new Believer now has the responsibility to ***make time*** to spend with the HS on a consistent basis. This point is non-negotiable!

This is where the HS mentors you and helps you to grow in maturity and sharpen your sense of contrition through the spirit of ***recognition, repentance and reconciliation.*** It is critical that the Believer immerse himself in prayer and meditation to learn to "hear" (see in the spirit) what the Spirit of the Lord is saying ***because men don't come to the light unless their sins are exposed!***

This is a vital step in the development of the spiritual man because the person who is immature (carnal) in Christ cannot make decisions on things he does not understand. The apostle Paul exhorts us not to receive the grace (warnings) of God in vain with great conviction in 2 Corinthians 6:1-10 as he outlines the present realities of life in ministry:

"We then, as workers together with Him also plead with you not to receive the grace of God in vain. For He says: "In an acceptable time I have heard you, and in the day of salvation I have helped you." Behold, now is the accepted time; behold, now is the day of salvation. ***We give no offense in anything, that our ministry may not be blamed.***

But in all things we commend ourselves as ministers of God: in much patience, in tribulations, in needs, in distresses, in stripes, in imprisonments, in tumults, in labors, in sleeplessness, in fastings; by purity, by knowledge, by longsuffering, by kindness, by the Holy Spirit, by sincere love, by the word of truth, by the power of God, by the armor of righteousness on the right hand and on the left, by honor and dishonor, by evil report and good report; as deceivers, and yet true; as unknown, and yet well known; as dying, and behold we live; as chastened, and yet not killed; as sorrowful, yet always rejoicing; as poor, yet making many rich; as having nothing, and yet possessing all things."

Grace (warnings) and the thorn (afflictions) reflect the ambivalence of ministry and the indisputable crisis that awaits every person who accepts the mantle of salvation and the accompanying marks of ministry to the Glory of God. In the final analysis, the key element to devoted passionate service in the KOG is ***endurance.*** Amen.

The Spirit of Integrity

"He who walks with integrity walks securely, but he who perverts his ways will become known."

(Proverbs 10:9)

Integrity, like all things, is a spirit. It is *the quality of being honest and having strong moral principles; moral uprightness.* In Hebrew the word is *(tom, tummah)* and is translated to mean simplicity, soundness, completeness, (to be) upright and perfection.

It reflects the sincerity of heart and intentions. It projects truthfulness and is one of the words ***(thummin: which is the plural of integrity)*** that was engraved on the breastplate of the high priest in the OT (Exodus 28:30). Integrity is one of the fundamental cornerstones of true spiritual character.

That being said, ***when is the last time your faith has been in a fight?*** Christians in the West have become "soft." They lack spiritual integrity because they don't spend enough time with God, lack holiness and they bail out on fiery trials which causes their faith to be lackluster. Christians are soft because they have been taught to connect with the ***body*** (seek man's advice) before connecting with the ***Head*** (seeking the face of God). We get consumed by what we are going through. We have all been Peter (the apostle) so many times, but we cannot stop pressing through our own self righteousness until we get into the Presence of God.

The integrity of the BOC is manifested in its response to adversity (tests and trials). In many cases, once a "church" goes from being an individual to becoming a building, it (the church) becomes useless to man. The building (and its ensuing financial burden and upkeep) becomes the priority within the ministry and everything else (God's people in the marketplace) takes a back seat.

Most Christians will not go where God wants them to go voluntarily. You can't volunteer for salvation. We want the promises but not the processes of God. One of the things that frustrates immature Christains is that ***the target keeps on moving*** (the enemy is creative in the different ways he comes at you).

All that a life of faith produces is the purpose to stay ***"green."*** When you are green, you still have room to grow some more. Don't be ***ripe***; the next step after being ripe is being ***rotten.***

Don't wait until you get into trouble before you seek the face of God. If you make the choice to pursue a relationship with God and become filled with the HS, you must be prepared to submit to His authority and be led wherever He takes you. In essence, you are switching from the driver's seat to the passenger seat in the spirit!

You need to welcome your tests and realize that ***you are only one bad experience away from being used mightily by God.***

The Spirit of Experience or Revelation

"Now we have received, not the spirit of the world, but the Spirit who is from God, that we might know the things that have been freely given to us by God."

(1 Corinthians 2:12)

Reality is redemption (not my experience of redemption). But redemption should reflect my conscious life. When I am born again, the HS takes me out of myself and my experiences and identifies me with Christ. I am led out of myself all the time. My experiences are not my reality, but the Reality (Christ) which produces the experiences.

My experiences must be Christ-centered. The HS cannot be put in a box and defined by your previous experiences. God will always take you back to the ***beginning*** *(His first encounter with you that you ignored or dismissed because you thought it was you producing the result or you just didn't understand what was going on).*

My relationship with Christ must always be paramount. I must be ruthless with myself when I am given to testimony and public witness about the experiences that helped to shape my spiritual realities. This is the foundation of faith and the revelation of Christ.

"The Crisis of Spirituality"

Faith that is sure of itself is not faith; ***faith that is sure of God is the only faith there is! Selah...***

Chapter Ten
The Spirit of Pressure and Patience

"My brethren, count it all joy when you fall into various trials, knowing that the testing of your faith produces patience. But let patience have its perfect work, that you may be perfect and complete, lacking nothing.

(James 1:2-4)

*"Pressure, in the spiritual sense, is **revelation** unveiled and then denied."* Faith can only appropriate to itself what the HS teaches it (faith). The main target of the imps and devils are Christian marriages. Marriage is the first institution that God created in order to sustain life and life more abundantly. Dismantling marriages is a key strategy by those fighting on the side of darkness in this bloody spiritual war.

The remedy to pressure is ***spiritual death (the execution of your will in the place of God's will)***. Pressure can also be interpreted as ***influence*** which is *the power to produce an effect by either direct or indirect means* (Acts 18:5) (2 Corinthians 4:6-12). Pressure is always prevalent (apparent) and is tantamount to ***suffering*** (2 Corinthians 11:21-29).

Patience and endurance have a symbiotic relationship in the life of a Believer. Troubles and difficulties are a major part of God's masterplan to develop our ability to withstand the tricks of the enemy and ***produce fruit*** (positive outcomes from grievous situations) and ***fruit that remains*** (manifesting a spiritual legacy in the earth realm that brings glory to God).

The testing of your faith means "tested" or "approved." The goal of testing is not to destroy or afflict, but to purge and refine. Patience transcends the idea of bearing (the weight or burden) of affliction; it upholds the mantle of remaining steadfast under pressure with a resolve that turns adverse situations into new opportunities for success, completion, wholeness and peace.

Believers must remember that the HS is our comfort (Comforter) in our sufferings and that we must develop patience under pressure for Him to lead us:

1. We must allow the HS into our most intimate and private places;
2. We must allow Him to make the most seemingly insignificant decisions;
3. We must yield to His power in business, politics, marriage, money, friendships, serving, finances, etc.
4. We must confess and repent to Him as Christ intercedes for us before the Father;
5. We must not grieve the HS with mundane and "dead worship" (Ephesians 4:30). Grieving the HS means to not push Him away, ignore or reject His counsel and Presence. Do not waste His time by continually asking Him for "stuff;"
6. We must seek Him first in everything (Matthew 6:33) and grace, power and the fruit of the Spirit will be given to us (Galatians 5:22-23).

The Spirit of Intimacy with the HS

"Nevertheless I tell you the truth. It is to your advantage that I go away; for if I do not go away, the Helper will not come to you; but if I depart, I will send Him to you."

(John 16:7)

This declaration from Jesus is a stark reality of the incredible advantage we have as Believers in the indwelling of the HS. It was a perilous assignment to follow Jesus in those days. ***Denial, suffering and even death*** were always right around the corner, so I can only imagine these jokers weren't too excited about Him leaving and them being faced with the prospect of possibly having to follow Him!

So Who was this Helper Jesus was referring to? Keep in mind that the disciples feared the presence of the Romans because they were viewed as disruptors of the peace and the Jews hated them because they saw them as blasphemers. The impartation of the HS had to be a difficult concept to comprehend at that time. How would the transfer of this Spirit take place? When would it happen and would it cause some sort of crisis in their spirituality which was incessantly under siege? They had longed for a Savior they could see, feel and touch, how could they become intimate with a spirit?

So Jesus explained the benefits of His departure by telling them that they would receive the Presence of the HS, the potential of full joy, the possibility of increased knowledge and revelation and the privilege of peace. Lastly, the Presence of the HS would be of more benefit to Believers than even the physical presence of Christ Himself since the Spirit would be able to dwell in all Believers at the same time.

Intimacy begins at the inception of the ***indwelling*** as the HS permeates your very being. Every cell in your body is captivated by His Presence! Think about the sacrifice Jesus made in giving up His position in the earth with us to give us something greater than Himself so that we could extend the love of Christ by engaging the world. All the promises of God are designed to give increase to the BOC as physical manifestations of the WOG.

God is telling us that the HS epitomizes His intimacy with us. He is saying, *"My HS is the demonstration of My power in you. Go ye therefore and make disciples."* God will bring conditions into your life that will either pull you in closer or push you farther away from His Presence. At that point, the choice for intimacy (fellowship) with the HS is all on you. The goal of ***chastisement*** (pruning) is to create intimacy with and dependence upon the Father.

At your confession of faith unto salvation, this is the first conversion which allows the flow of the HS in your spirit life. During the second conversion, which is the baptism of the HS, the Believer is equipped for service in the marketplace and must answer the compelling question, ***"Have you now become the sovereign possession of God?"***

Will you leave or will you follow? Selah...
The Spirit of Baptism

"Then Paul said, "John indeed ***baptized with a baptism of repentance****, saying to the people that they should believe on Him who would come after Him, that is, on Christ Jesus."*

(Acts 19:4)

The symbolism of the Christian baptism is a snapshot of cleansing and purification; of entering into the Presence of God one way (as a sinner) and coming out another way (as a son). Baptism is the initial public ***form of worship*** by a new convert and is a sign of a commitment to a new way of life as a Believer in the gospel of Truth.

There are two types of baptisms:

1) After salvation: ***Water is the elemen***t whereby the new Believer is baptized by the pastor, elders or deacons. Water is the ***witness*** to the confession of belief and to the repentance of sin; and,
2) Baptism of the HS: ***The HS and fire (trials and tribulations) are the elements*** whereby the new Believer is baptized by Jesus in the spirit. The HS is the ***witness and conduit*** by which the Believer is endued with power (dunamis) and spiritual gifts.

Baptism is a ***spiritual mass production*** of witnesses or ***"duplicates"*** of Christ. God knew that Jesus couldn't be everywhere at once, so He dispatched the HS to be the problem solver and fill the void in the lives of His sons in the earth. The HS is the only consciousness that truly knows the mind of Christ as they are One.

The HS fits us into a heavenly mold so that we can walk out the statutes of God in the marketplace. As the HS reveals Christ to us, the HS reveals us to Christ. The more of Him you have in you, the more you realize how much you need Him. As a witness for Christ, your actions will judge you; not a man, system or paradigm. Finally, the Believer is convicted by his sin by looking at Christ as the example of righteousness, holiness and peace. This is the Spirit of Baptism...

The Spirit of Spiritual Gifts

"Now concerning spiritual gifts, brethren, I do not want you to be ignorant: You know that you were Gentiles, carried away to these dumb idols, however you were led. Therefore I make known to you that no one speaking by the Spirit of God calls Jesus accursed, and no one can say that Jesus is Lord except by the Holy Spirit.

There are diversities of gifts, but the same Spirit. There are differences of ministries, but the same Lord. And there are diversities of activities, but it is the same God who works all in all. But the manifestation of the Spirit is given to each one for the profit of all: for to one is given ***the word of wisdom*** *through the Spirit, to another* ***the word of knowledge*** *through the same Spirit, to another* ***faith*** *by the same Spirit, to another* ***gifts of healings*** *by the same Spirit, to another the* ***working of miracles****, to another* ***prophecy****, to another* ***discerning of spirits****, to another* ***different kinds of tongues****, to another the* ***interpretation of tongues.*** *But one and the same Spirit works all these things, distributing to each one individually as He wills."*

(1 Corinthians 12:1-11)

One Spirit (the Holy Spirit) governs every activity in the KOG. Many Christians are in ***very poor spiritual condition***; therefore they must be built up in the Spirit through trials and tribulations. Because of the lack of interaction with and training by the HS, the following exchange is where most Christians have to stop in their conversation (witness) with those living in darkness seeking the light:

"...that if you confess with your mouth the Lord Jesus and believe in your heart that God has raised Him from the dead, you will be saved. For with the heart one believes unto righteousness, and with the mouth confession is made unto salvation." (Romans 10:9-10)

The inability to execute this simple act of love falls squarely on the shoulders of those individuals who call themselves Christians but are clearly living outside of the KOG. The bastardization of salvation has become a numbers game in the modern day church. *"How many people got saved today? **Only** three souls were added to the BOC."* The individual making the declaration, "only" has obviously been delinquent in their fellowship with the Father! The dispensation of spiritual gifts is a perpetual sign that God is still obsessed with the BOC this very moment and they are given to us for the ***profit*** (increase in wisdom and revelation of the knowledge of God and the manifestation of power, authority and rulership in His earthly kingdom) of all people in the marketplace.

Spiritual gifts have become a sort of competition in modern day Christendom and have corrupted the influence, integrity and witness of the institutional church. It is a grave mistake to pursue the ***"giftings"*** over the pursuit of your destiny. Sadly enough, far too many Christians in the BOC are indifferent toward cultivating their spiritual gifts because of ignorance and being consumed by ***idol worship*** (worshipping anything other than God).

Through spiritual gifts, the anointing of Christ flows from the Head to the BOC. Much of what we see in today's modern church is ***entertainment based*** Christianity (propping up the gifts like a cheap magic trick) whereby the church leaders are ***selling polluted bread as fresh baked bread*** to the masses. The consumption of polluted bread is contaminating the BOC and has diluted its appeal to thousands of people who are in pain and suffering. This crisis is spiritual treason and is creating a mass exodus of lost souls from the BOC.

The faith of Moses and other patriarchs caused a shift in the corporate dynamic; a "coming out" spiritual party of sorts where the true manifestation of gifts and talents was transferred from one individual to an entire body and the birth of prophets, priests and kings greatly enhanced the Presence of God in the earth. Now, all the attributes of Christ (Priest, Prophet and King) are compressed into one body (the BOC) with the result being the creation of a corporate army of soldiers ready, willing and able to extend the love of Christ to God's people in the marketplace .

The true wonder of the power of spiritual gifts is that they expose the greatest gift of all; **LOVE**. The WOG calls love, ***"a more excellent way"*** (1 Corinthians 12:31). All gifts come from God and are spiritual and all love comes from God and should flow through the gifts.

There are two types of love: ***natural and spiritual.*** Natural love is a standard operation between human laced selfish desires and carnal emotions. But a spiritual love is not selfish and God centered and is not used for personal edification.

The Spirit of Elisha

"A certain woman of the wives of the sons of the prophets cried out to Elisha, saying, "Your servant my husband is dead, and you know that your servant feared the Lord. And the creditor is coming to take my two sons to be his slaves." So Elisha said to her, "What shall I do for you? Tell me, what do you have in the house?" And she said, "Your maidservant has nothing in the house but a jar of oil."

"The Crisis of Spirituality"

Then he said, "Go, borrow vessels from everywhere, from all your neighbors—empty vessels; do not gather just a few. And when you have come in, you shall shut the door behind you and your sons; then pour it into all those vessels, and set aside the full ones."

So she went from him and shut the door behind her and her sons, who brought the vessels to her; and she poured it out. Now it came to pass, when the vessels were full, that she said to her son, "Bring me another vessel." And he said to her, "There is not another vessel." So the oil ceased. Then she came and told the man of God. And he said, "Go, sell the oil and pay your debt; and you and your sons live on the rest."

(2 Kings 4:1-7)

In the Book of 2 Kings there is a prolific story of tragedy versus remedy, lack versus excess and vision versus sight. It is the perspective of the reader that can change the situation of the person under siege. It has always been the case that the Lord God has fully utilized the ultimate behavior modification spirit of ***"adversity"*** to motivate His children toward the choice of life or death.

The Believer is thrust into the midst of the fire to burn off the "dross" of apathy, laziness and fear. Like the widow in this story when faced with the defining moment of her survival, the question will always come back to this, ***"What do you have in your house?"*** In that very instance, your ***"house"*** is not your place of residence, but rather, your ***"physical body."*** In other words, God is asking us the hard questions, *"What have I instilled in you?"* and *"Do you have the faith to believe Me for whatever you need? or "Will you continue to serve Me even in tribulation?" and "Will you submit to My chastening in order to produce glory for Me in the sight of non-Believers?" or "Are you a living sacrifice on the altar of God?"*

It's a hard thing to have ***"one foot in the grave and the other on a banana peel"*** and remain steadfast in the faith. The widow had the answer to her problem right in front of her face, but her "eyes"defied her. She was looking with natural versus spiritual eyes. She replied to Elisha, *"Your maidservant has **nothing** in the **house** but a jar of **oil.**"* Imagine that? She had nothing but oil! The prophet Elisha (is a ***"type"*** of Christ) and represents the spiritual encounter a Believer can have with the Father while walking in faith.

Are you an empty vessel?

She sent her sons out to collect "vessels" as directed by Elisha. She filled the pots with oil. The ***"oil"*** represents the anointing. The ***"anointing"*** is the ***"creativity of God."*** So the sons collected many vessels and filled them with oil inside the ***house** (this represents the **birth of faith** inside the heart, mind and soul of a Believer).* The widow sold the oil, paid off her debts and she and her sons lived off of the profits from the rest. End of story right? Nope...not by a long shot!

The ***empty vessel*** is a critical element in this story. In the Hebrew language, "vessel" is translated ***"keliy"*** (kel-ee: Strong's #113627); which is a vessel or a weapon; a thing (or person) prepared, perfected and completed to do work in the Kingdom of God.

A vessel that is full cannot be filled. Therefore, it is critical for Believers to constantly ***"pour out"*** of the abundance of their spirits to serve the life of one or more of God's people in the marketplace. The sons of God must view themselves as weapons that will boldly advance the KOG in the earth! We must remain in a constant state of pouring out so that the "oil" or the "creativity of God" will continue to flow through our witness to those living in the KOD. Empty vessels can only be filled by the Holy Spirit!

You do not want to be the son who comes into the Presence of the Father and states, ***"There is not another vessel"*** when the Father asks the question, ***"What do you have in your house?"*** Selah...

The Spirit of Transformation

"I beseech you therefore, brethren, by the mercies of God, that you present your bodies a living sacrifice, holy, acceptable to God, which is your reasonable service. And do not be conformed to this world, but be transformed by the renewing of your mind, that you may prove what is that good and acceptable and perfect will of God."

(Romans 12:1-2)

The "present" (wherever you are in real time) is where the place of transformation begins. Change in my own life is essential to my growth and maturity which enhances my ability to withstand spiritual crises. None of us have it at the inception of salvation, but in ***presentation*** (once you declare your commitment to the Lord in spirit) you are saying that you are altogether (completely and entirely) His and that you have given Him absolute authority over your life.

In this instance, God cannot only be your Savior and not your Lord. If that is the case, you will never experience true spiritual transformation. Transformation comes from a mindset that compels us to get into the Presence of God daily. Being in His Presence will change you; you should not ***"walk"*** like people who don't know Christ. No fruit in your life translates into boredom in the BOC.

The outward or carnal man (representing the spirit of Adam) is ignorant to the things of God. When his old nature enters the ***tomb***, (representing the spirit of repentance, reconciliation and redemption) he is crucified with Christ

and the Blood purges sinful things in you that you didn't even know about. The New Man emerges from the tomb reborn, filled with the HS and ready to share the Gospel of Truth with the sons and daughters of perdition.
The only way the ***"old man"***(representing the familiar, comfortable and sinful things we loved before Christ) can survive is if we go back to the grave (tomb) and dig him up.

The Believer must choose life (in Christ) or death (in Adam) by identifying his origin; tracing it back to God (Genesis 1:26) and not Adam. God will not allow any part of your old nature to remain. Examine the Gospel of Mark 6:41-45 and you will observe that God will always break what He takes, then He blesses it and after that He uses the thing He has blessed to meet the needs of others. This is the bedrock of transformation:

"This I say, therefore, and testify in the Lord, that you should no longer walk as the rest of the Gentiles walk, in the futility of their mind, having their understanding darkened, being alienated from the life of God, because of the ignorance that is in them, because of the blindness of their heart; who, being past feeling, have given themselves over to lewdness, to work all uncleanness with greediness.

But you have not so learned Christ, if indeed you have heard Him and have been taught by Him, as the truth is in Jesus: that you put off, concerning your former conduct, the old man which grows corrupt according to the deceitful lusts, and be renewed in the spirit of your mind, and that you put on the new man which was created according to God, in true righteousness and holiness."

(Ephesians 4:17-24)

"Blindspots" are obstacles placed in your life that need to be changed that others can see but you can't or won't acknowledge. Once your eyes have been opened, this occurrence represents the breaking point (or brokenness) where God can begin to use you. Reclamation of lost souls is the business of the HS as God reasserts His right and authority to gather His sons and daughters who are ***witnesses (duplicates)*** in the faith to Himself.

The Spirit of Time

"To everything there is a season,

A time for every purpose under heaven: A time [a]to be born, And a time to die; A time to plant, And a time to pluck what is planted; A time to kill, And a time to heal; A time to break down, And a time to build up;

A time to weep, And a time to laugh; A time to mourn, And a time to dance; A time to cast away stones, And a time to gather stones; A time to embrace, And a time to refrain from embracing;

A time to gain, And a time to lose; A time to keep, And a time to throw away; A time to tear, And a time to sew; A time to keep silence, And a time to speak; A time to love, And a time to hate;

A time of war, And a time of peace."

(Ecclesiastes 3:1-8)

All times are not the same, yet all time is relevant. The time of your birth was predetermined and pre-calculated by God in eternity to send you through a porthole in time as a seed to be tested, grow and mature as a son where you would be willing and able to walk out your destiny as a Kingdom citizen.

The anointing on an individual's life cannot be recognized or discerned by physical inspection; it must be revealed by the power of the HS. God breathes in worship and exhales revelation. Your revelation will be in direct correlation to your worship and sustains God in your life as a spiritual being.

People are birthed into a prearranged time (by God) to perform an act(s) to boldly advance the KOG. Just like everything else, ***time is a spirit*** and has several dispensations with varying degrees of functionality:

1. ***Prophetic Time (PT):*** is activated by a prophetic word (PW) or by a prophetic gift bestowed upon you by the HS. The PW might be spoken directly to you or into a season. Sometimes the PW may be released some time in advance of the occurrence and will begin moving toward you to meet you at a "***kairos***" moment in time (Isaiah 7:14). The PW and PT will intersect and the will of God will be done.
2. ***Overlapping Time (OT):*** is the dispensation of innocence, conscience, human government, promise, law, grace and the KOG era. These dispensations do not start and end on the same day; they overlap. God can do anything He wants to in an OT zone. Dispensation of the Law, Time Zone of Judges and the Prophets are in this dispensation. Nobody owns this time; it belongs to God. He can step into an OT zone and do what He wants to do. A great example of an OT zone is "***midnight;***" it doesn't belong to today or tomorrow.
3. ***Transitory Time (TT):*** when a person is in transit (going from one place to another); usually, a lesser place to a greater place where it looks in the "***natural***" realm like you are going backward but you are actually moving forward in the "***spiritual***" realm.
4. ***Seasonal Time (ST):*** is a time that reveals to us that only during certain seasons do certain things grow (manifest). In Obed-Edom (our ancestors were idol worshippers), we must sow in the right season. Sowing at the right time

will make any soil conducive to a bountiful harvest (seed, *time* and harvest).

5. ***Set Times (SeT):*** These are times God has set for a predetermined thing (Acts 1:5), (Psalms 110), (Psalms 75). The fullness of time cannot be altered or amended (Acts 4:4; ***"kronos"***: unfolding time (manifestation has not happened ***yet***); I don't have it now, but it ***is*** coming; ***"kairos":*** a moment in time when one's destiny is activated; the operative word in kairos time is ***"favor;"***
6. ***Spirit Time (SpT):*** this is significant in that all that was past and all that was future becomes present; right NOW! The operative word in spirit time is ***"acceleration."*** God will suspend time to bring you into your destiny (i.e. Moses at the burning bush (fire was burning but did not consume him) and Joshua (where God extended the daylight for him to defeat his enemies at Gibeon) (Joshua 10) and the advent of the HS in (Acts 2:1-4). All Gentile churches experienced spirit time. In (Romans 1:10-11), the HS is saying I must come and transfer my dominant gifts to you (because you are lagging behind) so that you will have what you need to move into your prescribed destiny.

Chapter Eleven:
The Spirit of Righteousness and Revelation

"Therefore I also, after I heard of your faith in the Lord Jesus and your love for all the saints, do not cease to give thanks for you, making mention of you in my prayers: that the God of our Lord Jesus Christ, the Father of glory, ***may give to you the spirit of wisdom and revelation in the knowledge of Him****, the eyes of your understanding being enlightened; that you may know what is the hope of His calling, what are the riches of the glory of His inheritance in the saints, and what is the exceeding greatness of His power toward us who believe, according to the working of His mighty power which He worked in Christ when He raised Him from the dead and seated Him at His right hand in the heavenly places, far above all principality and power and might and dominion, and every name that is named, not only in this age but also in that which is to come."*

(Ephesians 1:15:21)

Revelation is ***received*** easier than it is ***resisted*** (because the "old mindset" immediately resists anything new in the KOG). You cannot obtain a better life for you or your family from ***old*** (that is, "unsubstantiated") revelation (stale bread or a contaminated word). The KOG is an unveiling designed and created to bring discomfort to the Believer. None of the manifestations of the KOG can be afforded to me while I am ***"comfortable."***

Circumcision allows me to become the ***"word"*** I ***"hear."*** The apostle Paul defines true circumcision as a matter of the heart and not the flesh in (Philippians 3:3-11). He reveals three aspects of true circumcision:

1. Worshipping God in the Spirit,
2. Rejoicing in Christ, and
3. Placing no confidence in human honor or accomplishment as a means to reach God.

Circumcision paves the way for righteousness. Seeking the KOG and righteousness should be done simultaneously; it is not a two step process (Matthew 6:33). Righteousness is a character assessment and is the authority granted by Christ only to those who are citizens of the KOG. This authority power is given to the Believer as a result of fellowship with God and the accumulation of His wisdom and knowledge in order to discern the times.

Further, this authority power facilitates ***judgement*** (rulership, dominion and power over unrighteousness) whereby the Believer
governs his life according to the Constitution of the KOG (God's Holy Word). When the individual becomes focused on the WOG, sin and wickedness begin to fall off of him. A productive kingdom citizen will change the dynamic of the KOG through ***infiltration*** into the KOD. Infiltration can only be accomplished through action teamed with judgement influenced by revelation from God and discharged with righteousness.

The BOC is preoccupied with sin more than God is. One of the main focuses of revelation is ***"stretching"*** the saints into spiritual maturity. God will never stop stretching you, pruning you or chastising you (Isaiah 53:5).

The Spirit of Relationships

"Yet it shall not be so among you; but whoever desires to become great among you shall be your servant. And whoever of you desires to be first shall be slave of all. For even the Son of Man did not come to be served, but to serve, and to give His life a ransom for many."

(Mark 10:43-45)

Everything we do or don't do in life or everything we do or don't do for someone else is based upon our relationship with that individual. So to with God, establishing a close relationship with God will unlock the door to what ***He has already done for you.***

Relationships, or how we relate to one another, are based upon love (1 Corinthians 13:1-13). Love is the regulator and the standard for our interpersonal relationships. So then, the conclusion of the matter is centered around the Believer being "married" to the "ideal" of the person and not the "physical" embodiment of the person.

The Believer must maintain the spirit of consistency and normalcy in his "witness" (love manifested in passionate devotional service in the marketplace) in order to sustain a trusting and healthy relationship with others. The fruit of the Spirit must be apparent in the ideologies of the Believer. Come what may, those individuals in proximity to him/her (their "inner court") must not bear the brunt of their transgressions in order to validate the man or woman of God being affected by the external forces (spirits) dispatched to create turmoil in their lives.

In simple terms, do not take your frustrations out on someone you love and/or serve (Galatians 5:22). Amen.

The Spirit of Perception, Placement and Learning

"However, when He, the Spirit of truth, has come, He will guide you into all truth; for He will not speak on His own authority, but whatever He hears He will speak; and He will tell you things to come."

(John 16:13)

The perception of truth is a function and matter of ***placement*** (where you are situated spiritually in relationship to the HS). In the KOG, specifically, the BOC, you must be in the ***right place*** (where you can use your gifts to boldly advance the KOG). Your placement rides on the truth of who

Jesus is (your position or placement impacts your view) according to the WOG.

Sometimes it is hard hearing God in the earth realm because of the distractions of life; it is easy to lose focus. In order to hear God from heaven, the Believer must be poised, postured and ready to move strongly and decisively into an assignment from the throne room of Grace.

We have received a declaration to "come up" to the loftiness of Christ (Revelations 4:1) and dispatch carnal mindedness that seats us in lower places and to put on the spiritual mindset which elevates us to heavenly places. Life in Adam is a life in a lie because it rejects the deity of Christ and a life of love, peace and joy in the HS.

The BOC is fighting to stay in the grave (we must unction other Believers to discard their grave clothes) and replace hope with faith. Hope deferred makes the heart sick and stifles the divine process of learning ***(spiritual transformation).*** Jesus Christ is the goal of our learning which can be accomplished by maintaining focus on Him as the prime directive and experiencing Christ as He is unveiled in us. Spiritual transformation of the Believer is critical to the advancement of the KOG, so we can become ***the functional hand of Christ in the earth.***

These are the stages of the Divine Learning Process:

- Information: knowledge from experience
- Illumination: shining the light of the HS on the WOG in you
- Revelation: manifestation of divine impartation or divine truth
- Inspiration: revelation of the living WOG or peace, love and joy
- Realization: comprehension and processing of something
- Transformation: total destruction, then total reconstruction of the spirit man

- Representation: serving as a delegate for Christ

If you keep failing in the same place it is because you don't have a WOG to speak into that particular situation. You must ***know*** what is written and, more importantly, ***trust*** it. The truth comes through Christ who utilizes the HS to teach us the Living Word which leads to inspiration and manifests as passionate devotional service in the marketplace. The problem is not the lack of Word, it is the inability of the WOG to move the BOC from the ***"world mindset"*** into the KOG mindset.

OBEDIENCE + JOY = INSPIRATION

"But be doers of the word, and not hearers only, deceiving yourselves. For if anyone is a hearer of the word and not a doer, he is like a man observing his natural face in a mirror; for he observes himself, goes away, and immediately forgets what kind of man he was. But he who looks into the perfect law of liberty and continues in it, and is not a forgetful hearer but a doer of the work, this one will be blessed in what he does." (James 1:22-25)

Christians are feverishly copying the nature of Adam (his sin nature). Those living in darkness cannot see the Light (Christ) in us because of the veil (fear, sin and doubt) that covers us like a blanket. Once we immerse ourselves in the WOG, the veil becomes rent (torn away) by the HS and we begin to live a victorious life in Christ.

The Spirit of Leadership

"All Scripture is given by inspiration of God, and is profitable for doctrine, for reproof, for correction, for instruction in righteousness, that the man of God may be complete, thoroughly equipped for every good work."

(2 Timothy 3:16-17)

Timothy clearly states in this scripture that the leader chosen by God must be skilled in the WOG which will afford him the tools necessary to process information, judge difficult situations and render sound direction for God's people to follow.

The spirit led leader steps into chaos to bring order as God is methodical and has a divine purpose for everything He does. Too many Christians walk in the nature of Adam which is the spirit of rebellion. The ministry of salvation has been built on grace and mercy through submission, which is your power source in the KOG.

Leaders must reproduce Christ in the earth. Reproduction is the order of God and eminantes from ***marriage*** (as we are the bridegroom of Christ).The future of the blade of grass is inextricably tied to the integrity of the ***seed*** (the WOG) and the ***ground*** (lives of those people living in darkness) to which it is sown. Spirit led leadership will reflect the image of Christ while poor leadership will align itself with the old mindset (of Adam). Leadership must yield itself to the shifting of God.

Independent spirits exist within the BOC but will never prosper because they are ***out of order*** (diametrically opposed to the WOG). American culture and the modern day church have magnified the ***"deception of originality;"*** originality is not an attribute of a bonafide kingdom citizen or the Grace KOG. The KOG promotes transference and "succession" (or continuation) not "originality."

Jesus carried the seed of His Father's Spirit. That same Spirit has been reproduced in every Believer that has received Christ as Lord and Savior. The HS is a Seed. That Seed is incorruptible (1 Peter 1:22-23). The conclusion of the matter is this: the KOG is boldly advanced through faith, adversity and reproduction. Amen.

The Spirit of the Cave

"David therefore departed from there and escaped to the cave of Adullam. So when his brothers and all his father's house heard it, they went down there to him."

(I Samuel 22:1)

In the Hebrew language, *"Adullam"* means *"refuge" or "retreat"* and is a spirit. The spirit of the cave was there for David to reflect, refresh and resurge back into battle against King Saul. Much like David, much of what we fear outside the cave does not follow us into the cave. So much of what we value (worship, covet) is tied up in nothing because we are shallow, selfish, stubborn and not naked. Adullam is the place of nakedness.

The cave is also a "type" or reflection of God. In Psalm 57, David encouraged himself and after that, the Spirit of God arose in him to strengthen him. He was aware of his enemies, but he knew that God would fight his battles. He is so confident, in fact, that he began to sing and make music. He is so excited about his encounter, he declared that, "his spirit will wake him up early enough for him to awaken the dawn." ***David caught the revelation that he was going to awaken the One who never sleeps nor slumbers!*** You have to be dead to miss that!

The Spirit of the Covenant

"Greater love has no one than this, than to lay down one's life for his friends."

(John 15:13)

No greater love can be demonstrated than that which was manifested between God and mankind through the Blood of Christ. Covenant or "cutting or dividing"(***diatheke*** in Greek) signifies an unimaginable sacrifice made by Jesus to step out of eternity into time and die for a people who despised Him. It is the time where the Believer decides whether he is all the way in or all the way out of fellowship with the Father.

God's objective is to cause me to revisit my foundation (my life in Christ) not my condemnation (my life in sin). The covenant is the bridge for the BOC and the creation of a global family of Believers dedicated to boldly advancing the KOG. The "natural" family is in trouble because of what we have built our foundation on.

In Genesis 17:6-7, God makes His covenant with man and His covenant is not based upon convenience. God will send adversity (a shaking) to test your commitment to the covenant. In spirit terms, it is an irrevocable promise from God or mutual undertaking between parties where one or more binds himself to an obligation fully.

Chapter Twelve
The Spirit of Love

"A new commandment I give to you, that you love one another, even as I have loved you, that you also love one another. By this all men will know that you are My disciples, if you have love for one another."

(John 13:34-35)

There is no crisis in love because love is a product of the Spirit where Jesus is trusted. There is also no crisis in trust. Trust falls squarely on the side of an individual's "track record" with another person that quantifies the ***"trust equation":***

TIME + TRIALS x TRIBULATIONS - TESTAMENT = TRUST

The HS can and must be trusted because of His long standing track record of ***delivering*** *(coming through in clutch, making a way out of no way, providing a ram in the bush, etc.)* the beloved through trials and tribulations.

Jesus is the embodiment of love and love as a spirit is a compelling story of the "living death" that affords us the opportunity to suffer with Christ but not die! His love has embraced and transcended the ages from eternity into time. As I examine the spirit of love, I was led to this scripture as the preamble to the "zoe"(the rich, abundant, divine nature of God) kind of life:

"The [reverent] fear of the Lord [that is, worshiping Him and regarding Him as truly awesome] is the beginning and the preeminent part of wisdom [its starting point and its essence], And the knowledge of the Holy One is understanding and spiritual insight."

(Proverbs 9:10/AMP version)

The HS is utterly committed to creating glory for Jesus to be glorified. The triune Godhead operates in a synchronized manner to edify the BOC and bring glory to God Almighty. Love is an enigma. Love, in its most aberrant form, baffles the mind, crushes the heart, cripples the body and eviscerates the soul. Conversely, love is an all consuming fire which captivates the heart, mind, body and soul and merges them into one inescapable truth; this is the Lord's doing and it is well pleasing in His sight.

Why does a person remain in an abusive relationship? How can a mother exhaust every financial resource time and time again to bail her wayward son out of jail? Can you imagine the ***resolve*** (spirit of love) it takes to "raise" your grandkids because your daughter is hooked on drugs? The short answer is love. Love causes separation and unity simultaneously. It separates you from darkness and then unifies you with (in) the Light (Christ). The spirit of love is unfathomable. Love does what it does...it loves.

Look at the revelation Peter received in (1 Peter 4:1-8) from the HS regarding Christ as our example of love:

*"Therefore, since Christ suffered for us in the flesh, arm yourselves also with the same mind, for he who has suffered in the flesh has ceased from sin, that he no longer should live the rest of his time in the flesh for the lusts of men, but for the will of God. For we have spent enough of our past lifetime in doing the will of the Gentiles—when we walked in lewdness, lusts, drunkenness, revelries, drinking parties, and abominable idolatries. In regard to these, they think it strange that you do not run with them in the same flood of dissipation, speaking evil of you. They will give an account to Him who is ready to judge the living and the dead. For this reason the gospel was preached also to those who are dead, that they might be judged according to men in the flesh, but live according to God in the spirit. But the end of all things is at hand; therefore be serious and watchful in your prayers. And above all things have fervent love for one another, for **"love will cover a multitude of sins."***

So ***it is not our love*** that covers the transgressions of ourselves or others, but ***it is the love of Christ in us*** that compels us to do the unthinkable or irrational things we do to try and save someone we love or even a complete stranger. Evil acts or thoughts do not always suppress our emotions. Times of peace are often interjected with turmoil and conflict. The pressures of life impact people differently; some can cope with the grind while others cave in to feelings of desperation and chaos. But there is an incredible gift, an ***oasis of love*** given to those who believe in Him in the person of the Holy Spirit. Shalom.

The Spirit of Discipline

The result of ***discipline*** (*the practice of training people to obey rules or a code of behavior, using punishment to correct disobedience)* is freedom. There is a profound element of freedom in setting aside those things which cause a burden in the life of a Believer. Punishment can be considered "grace" when death is more likely the deserved penalty when the over zealous Believer strays off course in his daily battles with sin. One of the most compelling components of discipline is the posture of the Believer during ***worship*** (fellowship with and service to God and God's people in the marketplace). Jesus' most effective model of teaching was manifested during worship with the Father and through His service to the lost in marketplace ministry.

The spirit of discipline and ***rest*** are inextricably tied to one another. What is rest? Rest is not using your own strength, which is translated as ***favor*** in the KOG, and is when God causes someone else's resources, power, talent and influence to work on your behalf. God's seventh day was set apart for His rest. The number seven (7) represents perfection and completion and constitutes ***"the work that has already been done."***

Your destiny was conceived and birthed in eternity from the foundation of the world. Your destiny was distanced from the spirits of worry, doubt and fear. Your destiny has the ability to hear the voice of God and respond according to your faith. Your destiny is sanctified (blessed by the Lord and set aside for service). Wait a minute! Am I saying that your destiny is directly committed to a life of service in the KOG? The answer is, "Yes!"

The Spirit of the Lord is saying, "I have already set folks up to bless you if you remain disciplined, rest in Me (without worry) and walk out your destiny in faith, peace and love. Amen.

Scriptures on Spirituality

Philippians 3:10-14
That I may know Him and the power of His resurrection and the fellowship of His sufferings, being conformed to His death; in order that I may attain to the resurrection from the dead. Not that I have already obtained it or have already become perfect, but I press on so that I may lay hold of that for which also I was laid hold of by Christ Jesus.

Romans 8:5-9
For those who are according to the flesh set their minds on the things of the flesh, but those who are according to the Spirit, the things of the Spirit. For the mind set on the flesh is death, but the mind set on the Spirit is life and peace, because the mind set on the flesh is hostile toward God; for it does not subject itself to the law of God, for it is not even able to do so...

Romans 8:12-13
So then, brethren, we are under obligation, not to the flesh, to live according to the flesh— for if you are living according to the flesh, you must die; but if by the Spirit you are putting to death the deeds of the body, you will live.

Galatians 5:16-17
But I say, walk by the Spirit, and you will not carry out the desire of the flesh. For the flesh sets its desire against the Spirit, and the Spirit against the flesh; for these are in opposition to one another, so that you may not do the things that you please.

Ephesians 5:18
And do not get drunk with wine, for that is dissipation, but be filled with the Spirit,

"The Crisis of Spirituality"

2 Corinthians 3:18
But we all, with unveiled face, beholding as in a mirror the glory of the Lord, are being transformed into the same image from glory to glory, just as from the Lord, the Spirit.

Romans 8:29
For those whom He foreknew, He also predestined to become conformed to the image of His Son, so that He would be the firstborn among many brethren;

1 John 3:2-3
Beloved, now we are children of God, and it has not appeared as yet what we will be. We know that when He appears, we will be like Him, because we will see Him just as He is. And everyone who has this hope fixed on Him purifies himself, just as He is pure.

Romans 8:14-16
For all who are being led by the Spirit of God, these are sons of God. For you have not received a spirit of slavery leading to fear again, but you have received a spirit of adoption as sons by which we cry out, "Abba! Father!" The Spirit Himself testifies with our spirit that we are children of God,

Galatians 4:6
Because you are sons, God has sent forth the Spirit of His Son into our hearts, crying, "Abba! Father!"

Galatians 5:22-23
But the fruit of the Spirit is love, joy, peace, patience, kindness, goodness, faithfulness, gentleness, self-control; against such things there is no law.

Matthew 7:17
So every good tree bears good fruit, but the bad tree bears bad fruit.

"The Crisis of Spirituality"

John 15:5-8
I am the vine, you are the branches; he who abides in Me and I in him, he bears much fruit, for apart from Me you can do nothing. If anyone does not abide in Me, he is thrown away as a branch and dries up; and they gather them, and cast them into the fire and they are burned. If you abide in Me, and My words abide in you, ask whatever you wish, and it will be done for you.

Romans 14:17
For the kingdom of God is not eating and drinking, but righteousness and peace and joy in the Holy Spirit.

Ephesians 5:8-9
For you were formerly darkness, but now you are Light in the Lord; walk as children of Light (for the fruit of the Light consists in all goodness and righteousness and truth),
1 John 4:7
Beloved, let us love one another, for love is from God; and everyone who loves is born of God and knows God.

John 13:34-35
A new commandment I give to you, that you love one another, even as I have loved you, that you also love one another. By this all men will know that you are My disciples, if you have love for one another."

1 Corinthians 13:1-4
If I speak with the tongues of men and of angels, but do not have love, I have become a noisy gong or a clanging cymbal. If I have the gift of prophecy, and know all mysteries and all knowledge; and if I have all faith, so as to remove mountains, but do not have love, I am nothing. And if I give all my possessions to feed the poor, and if I surrender my body to be burned, but do not have love, it profits me nothing.

"The Crisis of Spirituality"

***Colossians* 3:12**
So, as those who have been chosen of God, holy and beloved, put on a heart of compassion, kindness, humility, gentleness and patience;

***1 Corinthians* 3:1–3**
And I, brethren, could not speak to you as to spiritual men, but as to men of flesh, as to infants in Christ. I gave you milk to drink, not solid food; for you were not yet able to receive it. Indeed, even now you are not yet able, for you are still fleshly. For since there is jealousy and strife among you, are you not fleshly, and are you not walking like mere men?

***1 Corinthians* 14:20**
Brethren, do not be children in your thinking; yet in evil be infants, but in your thinking be mature.

***Hebrews* 5:13–14**
For everyone who partakes only of milk is not accustomed to the word of righteousness, for he is an infant. But solid food is for the mature, who because of practice have their senses trained to discern good and evil.

***Galatians* 6:1**
Brethren, even if anyone is caught in any trespass, you who are spiritual, restore such a one in a spirit of gentleness; each one looking to yourself, so that you too will not be tempted.

***Romans* 14:1–3**
Now accept the one who is weak in faith, but not for the purpose of passing judgment on his opinions. One person has faith that he may eat all things, but he who is weak eats vegetables only. The one who eats is not to regard with contempt the one who does not eat, and the one who does not eat is not to judge the one who eats, for God has accepted him.

"The Crisis of Spirituality"

1 Corinthians 8:9-13
But take care that this liberty of yours does not somehow become a stumbling block to the weak. For if someone sees you, who have knowledge, dining in an idol's temple, will not his conscience, if he is weak, be strengthened to eat things sacrificed to idols? For through your knowledge he who is weak is ruined, the brother for whose sake Christ died.

Scriptures on Conflict

"Blessed are the peacemakers, for they will be called children of God."
Matthew 5:9

"You have heard that it was said, 'Eye for eye, and tooth for tooth. But I tell you, do not resist an evil person. If anyone slaps you on the right cheek, turn to them the other cheek also. And if anyone wants to sue you and take your shirt, hand over your coat as well. If anyone forces you to go one mile, go with them two miles. Give to the one who asks you, and do not turn away from the one who wants to borrow from you."
Matthew 5:38-42

"If your brother or sister sins, go and point out their fault, just between the two of you. If they listen to you, you have won them over."
Matthew 18:15

"So watch yourselves. "If your brother or sister sins against you, rebuke them; and if they repent, forgive them."
Luke 17:3

"A new command I give you: Love one another. As I have loved you, so you must love one another".
John 13:34

"In your anger do not sin" Do not let the sun go down while you are still angry..."
Ephesians 4:26

"Do not let any unwholesome talk come out of your mouths, but only what is helpful for building others up according to their needs, that it may benefit those who listen."
Ephesians 4:29

".....not looking to your own interests but each of you to the interests of others."
Philippians 2:4

"Do not repay anyone evil for evil. Be careful to do what is right in the eyes of everyone. If it is possible, as far as it depends on you, live at peace with everyone. Do not take revenge, my dear friends, but leave room for God's wrath, for it is written: "It is mine to avenge; I will repay," says the Lord. On the contrary: "If your enemy is hungry, feed him; if he is thirsty, give him something to drink. In doing this, you will heap burning coals on his head." Do not be overcome by evil, but overcome evil with good."
Romans 12:17-21

"Bear with each other and forgive one another if any of you has a grievance against someone. Forgive as the Lord forgave you."
Colossians 3:13

"See to it that no one falls short of the grace of God and that no bitter root grows up to cause trouble and defile many."
Hebrews 12:15

"Love is patient, love is kind. It does not envy, it does not boast, it is not proud. It does not dishonor others, it is not self-seeking, it is not easily angered, it keeps no record of wrongs. Love does not delight in evil but rejoices with the

truth. It always protects, always trusts, always hopes, always perseveres."
1 Corinthians 13:4-7

"My dear brothers and sisters, take note of this: Everyone should be quick to listen, slow to speak and slow to become angry, because human anger does not produce the righteousness that God desires."
James 1:19-20

"Finally, all of you, be like-minded, be sympathetic, love one another, be compassionate and humble. Do not repay evil with evil or insult with insult. On the contrary, repay evil with blessing, because to this you were called so that you may inherit a blessing. For, "Whoever would love life and see good days must keep their tongue from evil and their lips from deceitful speech. They must turn from evil and do good; they must seek peace and pursue it."
1 Peter 3:8-11

"Do not seek revenge or bear a grudge against anyone among your people, but love your neighbor as yourself. I am the Lord."
Leviticus 19:18

"The words of the reckless pierce like swords, but the tongue of the wise brings healing."
Proverbs 12:18

"A gentle answer turns away wrath, but a harsh word stirs up anger."
Proverbs 15:1

"The Crisis of Spirituality"

"When the Lord takes pleasure in anyone's way, he causes their enemies to make peace with them."
Proverbs 16:7

The Results of Life in the Spirit

The New Man

17 "This I say, therefore, and testify in the Lord, that you should no longer walk as the rest of the Gentiles walk, in the futility of their mind, 18 having their understanding darkened, being alienated from the life of God, because of the ignorance that is in them, because of the blindness of their heart; 19 who, being past feeling, have given themselves over to lewdness, to work all uncleanness with greediness.

20 But you have not so learned Christ, 21 if indeed you have heard Him and have been taught by Him, as the truth is in Jesus: 22 that you put off, concerning your former conduct, the old man which grows corrupt according to the deceitful lusts, 23 and be renewed in the spirit of your mind, 24 and that you put on the new man which was created according to God, in true righteousness and holiness."

(Ephesians 4:17-24)

"Sight is what you have when your eyes are open, vision is what you have when your eyes are closed!"

Ivan Kizza, Kampala, Uganda

March 2004

"The Crisis of Spirituality"

Notes

"The Crisis of Spirituality"

Notes

"The Crisis of Spirituality"

Notes

www.ingramcontent.com/pod-product-compliance
Lightning Source LLC
LaVergne TN
LVHW012104160826
845678LV00014B/2930

* 9 7 9 8 7 2 5 1 9 1 9 7 4 *